20 Way
Stand Out
Using Print

Get noticed and generate leads with a strategy most small businesses ignore

Keith Barker

Keefomatic

Keefomatic Studio
keefomatic.com

20 Ways to Stand Out Using Print

Published by Keefomatic Studio
keefomatic.com

ISBN: 978-1-0685915-0-1 (paperback)
ISBN: 978-1-0685915-1-8 (eBook)

Typeset in 9/14 Source Serif Pro by Adobe Systems
by Keefomatic Marketing & Design

Contents

Stay Inspired

Stay inspired and keep your marketing fresh! Sign up for the *20 Ways* mailing list to get exclusive tips, updates and resources to help your business stand out using print and beyond. It's free and easy to join, I promise to never sell your data, and you can leave at any time. Come and join us!

Introduction

Small businesses are resourceful by necessity. When it comes to marketing, most SMEs don't have a lot of money to throw around, and for many, their marketing budget is either tiny or non-existent. So what happens when you've got to get your name out there but don't have the funds? Many choose to go the DIY route.

With no budget to hire a professional, most business owners turn to the easiest, most accessible option – free social media platforms. It feels like the obvious choice. After all, everyone's on Facebook or Instagram, and it doesn't cost anything to post.

But there's a catch: with no budget for design or copywriting, small businesses tend to borrow ideas from those they see in the marketing around them. This often means taking inspiration from big name brand campaigns from companies we all recognise. These ads look slick and successful, so why wouldn't you try to copy them?

Unfortunately, this approach doesn't quite work the way SMEs hope. The truth is, free social media platforms and those major brand initiatives you're mimicking are mostly designed to create brand awareness.

The Limits of Brand Awareness

Brand awareness is about making sure people know who you are, and that's a good objective to have. However, for your brand to grow it relies on two things: your brand being present in customers' minds (mental availability), and your product or service being readily accessible when they want to buy it (physical availability).

For large companies, this works like a charm because they can afford to flood all sorts of media channels with their messaging. Whether it's billboards, TV or endless social media ads, they're everywhere. Plus, their products are widely available, which makes it easy for consumers to choose them when they're in the mood to buy.

For SMEs, though, it's a different story. You can't dominate media space because you can't afford to be everywhere. And even if you could, your products or services aren't as widely available as, say, a bottle of Coca-Cola or a packet of Walkers crisps. So, even if someone becomes aware of your brand, there's no guarantee they'll be able to find you or buy from you when they're ready.

Social Media and SEO Are Failing Small Businesses

For SMEs heavily invested in free social media and in search engine optimisation (SEO), there is a larger problem. These tools were once seen as cost-effective ways to reach new customers. But today, they are failing to deliver results for small businesses.

Social media platforms are overcrowded, and algorithms change constantly. Organic (non-paid) reach is in terminal decline. It used to be that a single post could engage your audience and lead to sales. Now, most of your posts are seen by a tiny fraction of your followers unless you pay to boost them.

SEO has followed a similar path. Competition to get your content listed on the first page of a Google search is fierce, and its algorithms now favour big brands and major publishers. For SMEs, it's getting harder to rank highly, especially with paid ads and AI-driven search features taking over the results pages.

As Rand Fishkin from SparkToro points out, SEO is now a game for big brands and established domains, not newer or smaller players.* In short, the old pillars of small business digital marketing – organic social media and SEO – are no longer reliable ways to reach new customers.

Instead of relying on declining social media and SEO tactics, small businesses need to rethink their approach entirely. The goal shouldn't be to replicate big-brand strategies, but to focus on lead generation using marketing channels that deliver direct, measurable results. For SMEs, it's not about being everywhere – it's about being where it counts.

We Need To Do Things Differently

So, where does that leave us? If copying big brands doesn't work, and widely-used digital tactics are losing their effectiveness, what is a small business supposed to do?

The answer is to diversify the marketing channels you use and shift your focus from simply being visible to actively generating leads.

- **Focus on Lead Generation**: For small businesses, getting in front of new customers is essential. While visibility is important, the real value comes from generating interest and converting that into sales. Tactics like referral programmes, local advertising or direct response marketing can help you find and attract potential customers, not just keep your name out there.
- **Marketing Consistency**: Regular, consistent marketing efforts are crucial, even on a smaller scale. Whether through email newsletters, networking or local advertising, staying active and engaged helps you keep a steady flow of leads coming in. The more consistent your efforts, the more reliable your results will be.

Whichever marketing channels you choose for your business, concentrating on getting more leads and treating marketing as an ongoing, continual process (not a disjointed collection of one-off projects) will help you grow.

That could mean investigating different marketing channels such as online or offline advertising, email marketing, sponsorship, exhibitions, networking, PR – whatever helps you find more customers. And another alternate channel is the subject of this book – print-based marketing.

---

* *https://sparktoro.com/blog/an-anonymous-source-shared-thousands-of-leaked-google-search-api-documents-with-me-everyone-in-seo-should-see-them/*

Print marketing offers small businesses a tangible, lasting way to reach their audience and generate leads. Unlike fleeting social media posts that hardly anyone sees, a well-placed flyer, brochure or direct mail piece can remain in a customer's home or office, serving as a constant reminder of your brand and prompting them to take action. Print can also help you cut through the digital noise, reaching people in a more personal and memorable way, encouraging them to engage with your business.

In the chapters that follow, we'll explore how you can use print marketing to grow your business – strategies that are not just effective but also tailored to the unique challenges and opportunities faced by small businesses.

From vehicle graphics to direct mail, print-based marketing might just be the breath of fresh air your business needs in a world that's increasingly focused on digital.

But before we embark on a journey through the world of print marketing, we need to address a common question.

Does Print Still Matter?

You're probably thinking: *Print marketing sounds a bit old-fashioned to me. Print is dead – everyone knows that.*

And you're right, or course. Once the backbone of commerce, print media has been overtaken. Today, with the entire internet at our fingertips, clinging to print is a waste of time. Print can't hope to beat digital media, and there are many reasons why.

Firstly, there's reach. When a single tweet can travel around the world in under a second, why limit your audience to those who happen to stumble upon your material?

Digital content is interactive, shareable and, most importantly, measurable. Want to know how many eyes saw your advert in yesterday's paper? Good luck with that. Need to see real-time engagement with your online ads? You can find that in just a few clicks.

Then there's the issue of sustainability to consider. In an era when the call to go green is louder than it's ever been, can we really justify the environmental impact of printing? The trees cut down for paper, the ink, the waste – it's a hefty price to pay for something that's increasingly seen as a relic.

We can't ignore cost-effectiveness either. Small businesses are always looking for ways to maximise their marketing budgets. With production, distribution and material costs, print spending soon adds up. Digital marketing, on the other hand, offers low-cost or even no-cost solutions that can be scaled up or down at a moment's notice, depending on your needs.

To those people still clinging on to the nostalgia of print, I get it. There's a certain romance to holding a tangible, physical document. But in business, sentimentality doesn't pay the bills – efficiency and effectiveness do.

It's time to completely embrace the digital age, not with a regretful backward glance but with a forward-facing determination to drive on into a brave new digital world.

For small business owners, entrepreneurs and marketing professionals, the message is clear: adapt to the digital revolution or risk being left behind.

I Thought This Was A Book About Print!

It is. You've probably heard arguments like these many times. But before we commit print media to the earth for a final time, let's examine this "Print is dead" argument with a critical eye, because it's not all it seems to be. Print media still has a whole host of advantages that digital media can only dream of.

Firstly, print is a tactile, sensory medium. In an increasingly virtual world, the physicality of printed media – the feel of a glossy magazine, the texture of high-quality paper, the smell of the ink – offers sensory engagement that digital formats can't compete with.

It's not about nostalgia – it's about impact and memorability. Print engages the senses and evokes emotions and memories in a way that a screen never will – emotions that can create a deeper, lasting, meaningful connection in the minds of your audience. It's for that very reason you don't send your significant other an email birthday card.

People claim they decide to buy products and services using cold logic, but that's not the case. Emotion is the key to unlocking their decision-making processes. And print evokes emotion.

When was the last time a pay-per-click ad made you emotional (apart from enduring the agony of trying to set one up, that is)?

And what about the cluttered digital landscape? With millions of tweets, posts, reels and ads bombarding us every single day, we are tired and digital fatigue is real.

People are unplugging their devices to escape the stress and negativity of endless screen time, aiming to improve their mental health and reconnect with the real world. There's a reason it's called "doomscrolling." The steep rise in people taking a digital detox shows that the digital revolution ain't all it's cracked up to be.

Regular people (i.e. your customers) are doing these detoxes and not coming back to social media. With privacy concerns, fake content, intrusive ad tracking and random account suspensions (with no prospect of ever speaking to a human to solve them), many of us are on the verge of ditching social media entirely.

Well-designed print marketing doesn't have to compete with a dozen other tabs or notifications. It doesn't track you. Instead, it captures and holds your attention in a way that digital struggles to match – offering a moment of undivided engagement in our dot-com-slash lives.

And then there's trust? Do you believe what you see on social media? Studies have shown that people trust information from print sources far more than digital ones.

In an era of deepfakes, deception and cut-n-paste AI content, the credibility and trust you get through the medium of print has never been more important. For small businesses and marketers, trust is like gold dust.

Print is inclusive. Despite growing internet access, not everyone prefers or has easy access to digital platforms. Print bridges this gap, reaching people across generations and those without reliable internet access, ensuring your message gets to everyone.

And claims about sustainability from digital advocates are pure hypocrisy. The print industry takes its environmental responsibilities seriously, from recycling programmes to sustainable forestry practices and developing vegetable-based inks. These advancements reflect a commitment to eco-friendliness that challenges the notion that print is inherently wasteful.

On the other hand, there are enormous environmental costs associated with an increasing reliance on digital media and technologies. From the obscene amounts of energy required by AI to the raw materials and labour practices that go into making every single memory chip – digital infrastructure, devices, data centres and networks account for between 6% and 12% of the *entire planet's* energy use.

When it comes to cost, the argument that print is prohibitively expensive doesn't hold water when you consider its long-term value and tangible impact. As Rory Sutherland of Ogilvy put it, "Print is vastly more effective than digital *because* it is more expensive." It signals a business that invests in itself and its message – spending on printed marketing demonstrates your commitment.

And cost comparisons with free-to-use social media are pointless. Relying on organic reach is now so ineffective that if you wish to target a wider audience, you have to spend on advertising. Free social media marketing, for most small businesses, is worthless.

Writing off print media in favour of an all-digital approach is not only premature, but also a misunderstanding of the unique value print brings to the marketing mix.

Its emotional appeal, sensory nature, focused engagement, trustworthiness, inclusivity and advances in sustainability all point to a medium bursting with life, not lingering at death's door.

Like most choices in life, the decision between print and digital should not be either/or.

For SMEs, entrepreneurs and marketing pros, the savvy move is not to abandon print but to integrate it smartly alongside your digital efforts, creating a marketing strategy that leverages the best of both worlds.

Why Print Endures in the Modern Marketing Landscape

While digital marketing offers impressive reach and in-depth analytics, print offers unparalleled intimacy and longevity. Successful marketing is about finding ways to combine them.

For example, our family garden design business uses Instagram to successfully showcase our garden transformations. But when a potential client books a consultation, they're also presented with a printed brochure featuring more stunning garden photography.

This coffee-table-style brochure becomes a keepsake, remaining long after the Instagram reels have come and gone. Here, print and digital aren't competing but collaborating, each amplifying the other's strengths.

Print marketing offers a tangible, intimate counterpoint to the transient nature of online content. For small businesses, integrating print into your marketing strategy can mean the difference between being noticed and being remembered.

Ultimately, it's about standing out and making a lasting impression. As we'll see, print has the power to do just that.

Why Did I Write This Book?

My mission is to assist my fellow small business owners to find more customers, stand out, and project a more professional image through the strategic and tactical use of design and marketing.

The bulk of this book began as an email series that I wrote in 2022 and was borne out of a realisation. I observed that many of my clients had begun to notice that social media had stopped working for them.

They were heavily invested in social media for their marketing – often to the exclusion of any other marketing activity – and their results were poor and getting worse. This book offers a fresh perspective and a different approach, which my clients are now using to improve their visibility.

I have nothing against social media. I use it myself. The trouble is, so does everyone else.

There are plenty of small business owners and marketers who don't remember a time without social media. The last twenty years has seen a dramatic evolution in marketing which some don't even realise has happened. As David Byrne once said: "*You may ask yourself, how did I get here?*"

For those who weren't around, here's a reminder.

Twenty Years of SME Marketing in Two Minutes

It's 2005. No smartphones, no Facebook. Back then, small business marketing relied on traditional, local promotion to get the word out. The high street was bustling, and many SMEs thrived by building strong local reputations.

Print media was king. Local newspapers and magazines were filled with display ads and classifieds. Flyers were stuffed through letterboxes, handed out in town centres or slipped under car windscreen wipers. Direct mail – dubbed "junk mail" – was everywhere.

While radio, TV, and billboards were out of reach for most SME budgets, community events, trade shows and networking were invaluable. Personal relationships were vital to building trust and growing your business.

Without Google in your pocket, being listed in printed directories like the *Yellow Pages* was essential for being found. A few forward-thinking businesses were starting to build websites and dabble with early digital marketing tools like Google AdWords, but for the most part, marketing remained a digital-free zone.

Then, in 2006, Facebook appeared, and everything changed. A year later business owners were invited to create company pages, opening the door to a new way of reaching customers. It was a gold rush – SMEs flocked to social media, excited by the promise of free marketing and direct customer engagement. The appeal was obvious – no budget required, increased visibility and the chance to build a community of loyal fans.

But the dream didn't last. As Facebook's user base exploded, its algorithms evolved. What was once a chronological feed became a tightly curated stream of content. Organic reach – the number of people your posts reached for free – plummeted.

Today, Facebook's organic reach averages 2.6%. If you have 200 followers, that means only 5–6 people may see a particular post. In stats from 2023, the average number of post interactions for company pages with 1–1,000 fans was just *four*. Algorithms prioritise paid content, and attempts to direct users off-platform are penalised.

If you have below 1,000 followers, using Facebook for marketing is hardly worth the effort unless you're willing to pay. The promise of building an online community without spending heavily on ads is now a distant memory.

And it's not just Facebook. Instagram's organic reach is estimated to be between 1% and 4.5%[‡] and on LinkedIn it's 2.4–6.4%*. SMEs have been left struggling to adapt, as what once seemed like a digital marketing revolution now feels broken beyond repair.

Many businesses that thrived on free or low-cost digital exposure are now forced to spend more on marketing just to stay visible. Naturally, many aren't thrilled about it.

The Bait and Switch

It's hard not to feel like social media companies have pulled a classic bait-and-switch.

Initially, platforms like Facebook lured businesses in with the promise of free exposure. But once you were in, the rules changed – first subtly, then

---

‡ Instagram reach stats from SocialInsider

* LinkedIn reach stats from Social Status

drastically. Organic reach became throttled, with visibility tied not to the quality of your content but the size of your ad spend.

Sure, you can still use these platforms for free, but if you don't have a large following, the lack of reach makes it practically pointless. It's left many SMEs feeling frustrated, having poured huge amounts of time and effort into building their audiences only to find they can't reach them without paying for it.

This shift felt more like a ransom than a marketing expense, leaving a sour taste in the mouths of many small business owners. Social media platforms have morphed into freemium[1] models for businesses – free to use, but pay if you want actual results.

But There Is Another Way

As we've seen, businesses managed perfectly well to sell their services with little or no digital marketing twenty years ago.

I'm certainly not advocating for a return to those days. However, any decent marketing consultant will tell you that every business needs a robust marketing strategy based on multiple pillars. A sensible channel mix might look like:

- social media (free and paid),
- print media,
- in-person (i.e. networking/trade shows), and
- owned-media (i.e. blogging/email marketing)

This diversified list of activities is infinitely preferable to persevering solely with free, but dysfunctional, social media marketing and puts the power to reach new customers back in your hands.

---

[1] The list of Freemium software applications that started with a free-to-use model but have gradually removed or limited functionality to convert users to paid subscribers is a long one, and includes Evernote, Trello, Spotify, Dropbox, Zoom, Canva, Slack, Mailchimp and Hootsuite. While Facebook doesn't fit the traditional freemium model in the way some software applications do, its decline in organic reach has created a similar dynamic for businesses.

The View from The Cheap Seats

As Lieutenant Columbo (Google him, kids) used to say, "Just one more thing..."

I don't want to leave you with the wrong idea – there is value in paying for ads on platforms like Facebook, Instagram and LinkedIn. Their targeting tools are powerful, even if privacy laws have limited them a bit. If your audience is there, strategic paid ads can work. But here's the reality – the *free ride* is over. What used to be free is now a pay-to-play game, and it's time for SMEs to start budgeting for their marketing efforts again.

Over the last couple of decades, businesses have become accustomed to getting marketing and design for next to nothing. But that approach is no longer sustainable if you want real results.

The Shift Towards Free and Cheap Marketing

Twenty years ago, most marketing came with a price tag. A small *Yellow Pages* ad could cost hundreds of pounds, and even basic marketing materials like business cards were not cheap. Fast forward a few years, and suddenly businesses had access to free platforms like Facebook, where they could reach audiences at little to no cost.

This shift radically changed how SMEs thought about marketing. Why pay for brochures or print ads when you could directly target your audience online for free?

At the same time, design costs to businesses were slashed due to the emergence of crowdsourcing platforms like 99Designs and Fiverr, where anyone could get professional-looking logos and flyers designed at a fraction of the traditional fee.

But while these platforms saved SMEs money, they led to a race to the bottom for quality. Designers were forced to compete globally, with many working for wages so low they couldn't afford to put time or effort into the designs. The emphasis shifted from thoughtful, tailored creativity to fast, templated work that lacked originality and depth. Designers had to prioritise quantity over quality just to stay competitive, sacrificing research, concept development and refinement – critical steps in producing unique, effective work.

As a result, the end product often became formulaic, missing the distinctiveness and strategic thinking required to enable a brand to stand out. Over time, the widespread use of these services diluted expectations, conditioning businesses to accept "good enough" over truly exceptional design. Crowdsourcing undermined design as a profession, but it kept costs low for businesses – so the trend continued.

Design as a Commodity

The next blow for creative professionals came with the rise of DIY design tools like Canva. Businesses could now create their own professional-looking marketing materials using free or cheap templates. While Canva is a game-changer for SMEs on tight budgets, there's a catch – professional-looking doesn't always mean professional. Generic, template-based designs rarely capture the essence of your brand, and what's worse, everyone else is using the same tools, meaning your marketing merges into a sea of sameness.

As a result of all this – free marketing platforms, cheap crowdsourced design, DIY tools and templates – many SMEs grew accustomed to using low-cost or free solutions for their marketing and design, believing it was sufficient. However, in a competitive marketplace, truly making an impact demands more than just the basics.

The Shift Back to Paid Models

Now, as the digital landscape becomes more saturated and social media's free marketing bubble has burst, businesses must start budgeting for their marketing again if they want to stay visible.

Relying on free tools and platforms can only take you so far. Limited functionality, lack of customisation and cookie-cutter templates result in ineffective, forgettable marketing. To truly stand out, SMEs need to invest in strategic marketing efforts – whether through paid digital ads, print marketing or other promotional channels.

When Everyone Else Zigs, Zag

To break free and rise above the noise, businesses must invest where others don't. Paid advertising, print marketing, sponsorship and local events are less crowded spaces where your brand *can* stand out. With fewer competitors in these areas, it's easier to get noticed and remembered by your target audience.

Speaking of Brands

I talk a lot about brands, brand values and branding in this book, so let's clear up what I mean. There are plenty of definitions out there:

- Jeff Bezos: "Your brand is what people say about you when you leave the room."
- David Ogilvy: "The intangible sum of a product's attributes."
- Tom Peters: "A trust mark."

If the experts can't agree, it's no wonder small business owners get confused. Some think branding is just for big companies, but that's not true at all.

Your **logo** isn't your brand – it's just an entry point, like a cattle brand that marks ownership. **A brand is the image your business creates in people's minds**. That means different people may see your brand in different ways.

Your brand should reflect who you are, what you do and what you stand for – your vision, mission and personality. For SMEs, this often mirrors the owner's character. Good branding is about shaping how people think of your business, and poor-quality print, for example, can make your business seem cheap. In the end, branding is all about managing people's perception.

How To Read This Book

I always chuckle when authors tell you how to read their book, but if it works for them, who am I to argue?

The best way to read this book is... however you like. Binge it on a flight, read it in bed, or take it to the toilet – whatever works for you. My hope is you find something in here that will help your business, whether that's creating new touchpoints, standing out or selling more. If it helps you do any of that, then my job is done.

With over thirty years in print marketing, I've seen its power and effectiveness time and time again. Well-designed print has always been highly effective, and today's advances in digital printing have made it more affordable than ever.

This book is here to help you rediscover print as a valuable marketing tool - one that can help your business stand out, increase your sales and strengthen your brand.

What to Expect

This book is packed with practical marketing tactics. Each print item plays a unique role in an overall marketing strategy. I'll explain how each can be used to achieve different goals.

Some items may not be relevant to your business - if you don't have a physical store, you can skip the *Point of Sale* chapter, and if you don't sell products, the section on *Packaging* may not apply. Choose the sections that suit your business best.

The **20 Ways to Stand Out** are divided into three parts:

- **Quick Wins**: Easy, cost-effective print items that won't take weeks to prepare.
- **Stepping Up**: More involved projects that require a bit more investment but are well worth it.
- **The Big League**: High-impact projects that demand significant investment and collaboration with experts.

I've also included a few articles between sections to mix things up.

If you get some great results from any of these tactics, I'd love to hear about it - drop me an email at *keith@keefomatic.com*

Part 1

Quick Wins

When did any organisation (apart from the tax office) last write to you?

The disappearance of direct mail from our collective doormats gives you and your company a great big opportunity to stand out.

The same goes for printed loyalty cards. I used to go through paper loyalty cards from Caffé Nero almost every week, until they scrapped them in favour of an app – which only worked when it felt like it, if the signal wasn't patchy and it hadn't logged me out (not that I ever remembered my password anyway).

But honestly, it didn't come close to the simplicity of the paper version.

Printed loyalty cards are a straightforward and ludicrously cost-effective way for retail businesses to improve customer loyalty and generate returning business.

Direct mail and loyalty cards are a couple of prime examples of uncomplicated print marketing initiatives. They are straightforward, impactful activities that don't require a significant investment of time or resources, and yet, they are totally ignored by many businesses.

This section contains nine simple print wins, so (if you'll excuse the pun), let's press on.

These die-cut business cards, designed for cloud accounting firm Informed Accounting Solutions, stand out much more than standard business cards.

1

Business Cards

> Business Cards are perfect for creating brand awareness and making a lasting impression. They're essential at networking events, helping build your reputation and support PR efforts.

If you follow marketing discussions on social media (which I, unfortunately, have to), it won't take long to find a wet-behind-the-ears novice proclaiming that some tried and tested, traditional form of marketing is dead.

One week, it is blogging that's passed away (may it rest in peace). The following week it's advertising. Someone tried to persuade me that networking was dead the other day. (And while it was on life support during COVID, it's now sitting up, eating grapes and doing as well as can be expected.)

High on the list of things repeatedly pronounced extinct is the printed business card.

And, more often than not, the people declaring its demise are those hawking high-tech digital alternatives.

This is a book all about standing out. Electronic business cards only help you do that if you want to stand out as one of those people who assumes everyone is as tech-savvy as you are.

Electronic business cards are completely impersonal and instantly forgettable. They are also a privacy and security nightmare – why should I let your unknown random technology have access to my phone?

And at a more practical level, they all work differently. I don't know about you, but I don't have time to figure out what I'm supposed to do with someone's digital business card.

But it's a different story if someone presents me with their printed card. They are simple, inclusive (unlike digital cards), and just work.

For millennial marketers keen to keep things digital, it's also the work of a moment to include a printed QR code on the back that links straight to your website, mailing list or online shop.

An Exciting Opportunity

It's important to realise that business cards are much more than just carriers of contact information.

From a marketing standpoint, printed business cards offer an exciting opportunity to promote your brand values – opportunities that are simply impossible with a digital card. With a dash of creativity, you can make your business stand out and maybe inspire others with your unique approach.

Die-cutting – to create unusually shaped cards – can be very effective, especially if you can introduce some humour into them. If you imagine a bite mark out of one corner of a business card, that could be used by:

- a nutritionist
- a weight-loss coach
- a restaurant
- a dentist
- a cake shop

...and probably many other professions.

Utility Warehouse, the energy provider, used business cards shaped like piggy banks to encourage people to think about savings.

If your logo is approximately business card proportions, you can die-cut your cards to mirror your logo – as I did for one client who provides cloud accounting services. She now has cloud-shaped business cards.

One of my other business interests is a garden design firm. We thought of making business cards out of tiny seed envelopes, complete with flower seeds. You don't get that sort of creative imagination with a digital business card. You just get ones and zeros.

When I set up Keefomatic, my design and marketing business, my first cards were extremely fancy – silver ink on blind embossed thick black uncoated card, printed on a letterpress machine. They cost me an arm and a leg, but they were worth it for the interest they generated.

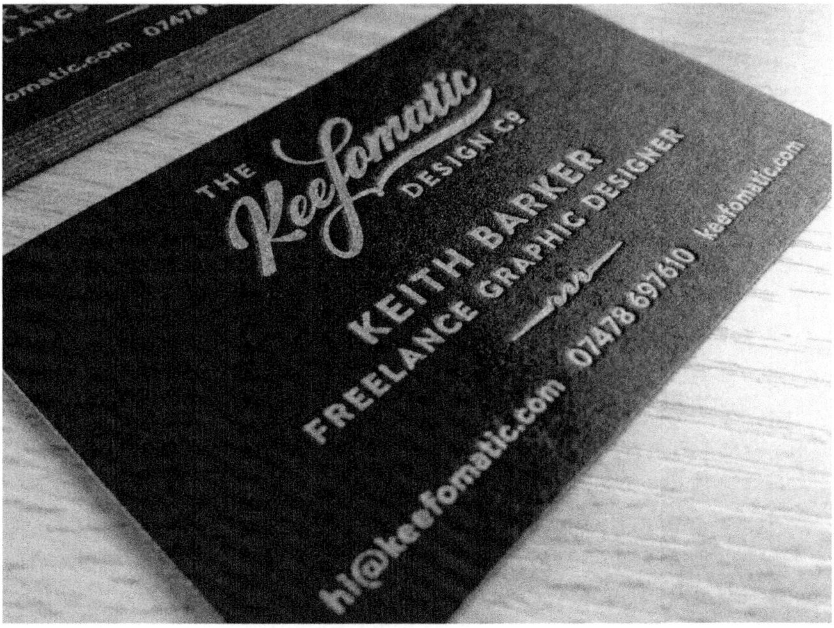

I had a new business and needed to make a splash, create a wow factor and set a high standard for quality. They certainly did that. When I visited a boutique creative agency in Nottingham, they told me my cards put theirs to shame!

You don't have to go to those extremes. Business cards are a cheap and effective way to create a buzz.

Many different paper types and finishes, such as velvet lamination, metallic ink or spot UV varnishes, can enable you to be a little different.

The paper you use tells a story about you and your brand. A business card printed on thick paper stock conveys confidence, while one on flimsy, uncoated paper says, "I'm cheap" (especially if it also says "Printed by Vistaprint" on the back).

Handing over your business card is often a potential client's first interaction with you and your brand. Your card's quality and attention to detail can help you make an unforgettable first impression, setting the stage for a successful business relationship.

And you know what people say about first impressions. Do you want to impress people or disappoint them?

The next time you hear someone tell you business cards are dead, remember that a traditional business card's tangible, personal and simple nature can speak volumes for your brand in ways an electronic one never will.

Key Takeaways

- Business cards are still relevant. They remain practical, memorable and effective.
- They are personal and tangible. Printed cards offer a human touch digital ones lack.
- Scope for creative branding – unique print techniques, designs, shapes or finishes can reinforce your brand.
- Adding QR codes allows you to link to websites, mailing lists or shops easily.
- Your selection of paper stock and finishes will reflect your professionalism, so choose carefully.
- High-quality cards set a positive tone and give a great first impression. Cheap cards cheapen your brand.
- Even premium cards are cost-effective to produce.

2

Letters

> Direct mail letters can generate leads and engage customers by delivering personalised messages. They're also great for driving sales, gathering feedback and educating your audience on new products, all while enhancing your brand's reputation.

The next three sections – letters, envelopes and postcards – are all forms of direct mail when combined, but each one offers unique possibilities on its own.

Some classic marketing tools have fallen out of favour, and one of those is the printed letter. Back in the late '80s, when I started in the design industry working at a printer in London, business stationery was our bread and butter. We printed reams of letterheads every week.

Then came one of London's infamous dialling code changes. The city scrapped 01 and replaced it with 071 for inner London and 081 for the suburbs. Businesses across the region scrambled to update their stationery – and then, not long after, the codes were changed again to 0171 and 0181. Chaos for business, but a goldmine for printers.

Of course, that was before the internet and email began the slow death of the business letter.

It's a shame, really. A beautifully crafted letter on premium paper is now a rarity. But this shift also creates an opportunity for you to stand out. In a world where inboxes are clogged with emails, receiving a personalised, signed letter can feel like something special.

And with modern printing technology, it's easy and affordable to create small, targeted batches of branded letters. You don't even need to print blank letterheads anymore – you can print both the letter and the letterhead in one go, complete with personalisation and a signature.

Think about sending a catalogue or brochure along with a signed, personalised letter. It's a small touch, but it can make a big difference. A physical letter feels more personal, more memorable, and with short-run printing you can print exactly what you need – no need for boxes of unused stationery cluttering up the office.

Why not write to your customers once in a while? Hardly anyone does anymore.

Something Unique

While I was writing this book I chanced upon a completely new and original product – **Pigeon**.

Pigeon markets itself as "letters reinvented". Pigeons are themed packs of six cleverly designed sheets of writing paper that fold to make their own envelope and are sealed closed with a postage stamp.

Each edition is designed by a commissioned illustrator, and the product was shortlisted for Gift of the Year 2024.

The creator, John Morse-Brown from Birmingham, designed Pigeon out of frustration with social media. He wanted a more meaningful way to stay in touch with distant friends and family, and so he combined his graphic design, engineering and origami skills to come up with this quirky product.

These self-contained letters hark back to the days when people wrote to each other regularly. They add back the emotion of receiving something that someone else has physically written – an emotion wiped out by electronic communication.

As their website puts it:

> *Find your favourite pen, a spot in the sunshine, and gently unfold the gorgeously illustrated paper to reveal the perfect frame for your thoughts, and a beautifully different way to show you're thinking of someone.*

Pigeons were designed for personal use, but SMEs and micro-businesses can also use them. In fact, when I wrote about these to my mailing list I had a number of replies from business owners telling me they'd bought some. I should have been on commission!

Writing to your customers individually, whether to thank them or to give them a special offer, will have enormous stand-out value – especially if your letter comes in one of these ingenious, eye-catching Pigeons.

You can visit the website at: *pigeonposted.com*

How Do You Write A Sales Letter?

This isn't a book on copywriting, but here are a few quick tips for writing an effective sales letter (many of these apply to website landing pages too).

First, decide how many letters you'll be sending. If it's just a few, you can make each one completely individual. But even for larger batches, personalisation is key.

Address your customer by name and acknowledge their specific needs or interests. This makes the letter feel more personal and relevant, rather than a generic sales pitch. If possible, reference a recent interaction or purchase to show you've taken the time to understand them.

When introducing your product or service, focus on the benefits, not just the features. Lead with how you can solve a problem or make life easier for your customer, and then back it up with proof. Use simple, clear language to keep your message compelling.

Highlight your unique selling point and, if possible, include a testimonial or short case study to add credibility. End with a strong call to action – make it clear what you want the reader to do next, whether that's visiting your website, calling for more information or redeeming an offer. And make sure the next step is easy, with all the necessary details provided.

Always finish with a thank you. A little appreciation goes a long way in leaving a positive impression.

For more detailed advice on sales letters, there are plenty of excellent books by people far more experienced than I am, including Dan Kennedy, Drayton Bird, Robert Bly, and the gloriously named Evaldo Albuquerque. There are a few mentioned in the Further Reading section.

Key Takeaways

- Printed letters are rare today, making them a standout way to connect with customers.
- Sending a personalised, signed letter feels special compared to crowded email inboxes.
- Modern printing allows you to create small, targeted batches without wasting stationery.
- Including a letter with a catalogue or brochure adds a memorable, personal touch.
- Products like Pigeon letters offer unique, creative ways to write to customers.
- Personalising letters with names and relevant details makes them feel more meaningful.
- A simple thank you in your letter leaves a lasting positive impression.

3

Envelopes

Envelopes help your brand and your message stand out from the moment they're received. They contribute to direct sales, lead generation and customer engagement.

It makes sense to follow letters with envelopes, and for this, we're going to step back in time once again.

The year was 1988. Kylie and Jason were at the top of the charts, and I was a poor student surviving on sachets of cup-a-soup while attending an art foundation course. The aim of this course was to undo everything we'd learned in school about art, which I was happily embracing despite my questionable diet.

One project stood out. We were asked to write a letter to a fellow student, create a custom envelope for it, and post it. Then, we had to take the envelope we received, decorate it further, and send it to someone else on the course. (I think the lecturers were making enthusiastic noises about random mark-making or Dadaism or something – the kind of stuff impressionable art students lap up.)

After a few rounds of this, our local postmen and women must have been getting pretty sick of us – but miraculously every letter was delivered, no matter how bizarre the envelope had become.

I'll save more of my art school reminiscences for my autobiography. This particular story is because we're talking about envelopes. Why? Because envelopes matter.

One of the key messages of this book is about standing out in business, and that includes doing things your competition isn't – like using creative envelopes for direct mail marketing.

In 1988, direct mail was so common it was often called junk mail. If you received a lot of it, it was common to separate your daily post into two piles:

A. To open now, and
B. To possibly open later (or put straight into the waste paper bin, depending on your mood).

Direct mail marketing companies knew the look of the envelope could make or break a campaign by increasing the mailer's chances of making it into Pile A.

Fast forward to today. How many pieces of mail do you actually receive each week? Probably not enough to create a pile, I'd imagine. But that's exactly why direct mail now offers a unique opportunity – hardly anyone does it anymore, so your message can easily cut through the digital noise.

How to Make Envelopes Work for You

Here's where we get practical. What can you do to ensure your envelopes stand out and get opened?

1. Use Colour to Your Advantage

The first and easiest thing to try is using coloured envelopes. Steer clear of brown – no one wants to be reminded of the tax office – but choose something eye-catching. If you've ever received marketing from me, you'll know it arrives in a lime green envelope. Why? Because it stands out and matches my brand. The moment it lands on your doormat, you notice it.

Think about your brand colours and how you can use them consistently in your mail. It's an easy, inexpensive way to reinforce your branding.

2. Think About Size and Shape

Most envelopes are a standard size – so why not play with that? Consider sending a smaller-than-usual envelope to pique curiosity. A tiny envelope, paired with a message like, "We can shrink your bills by 50%," is not going to be ignored.

Likewise, an oversized envelope might also do the trick. If it's too big to stack with the regular mail, it stands a better chance of being opened first. Just remember it will cost more to post.

3. Tease with Your Message

Printing on envelopes is affordable, and it gives you the chance to grab attention before the letter is even opened. Think of your envelope as an advertising space – print a teaser headline or intriguing question that makes the recipient curious. But don't give the whole game away. You want them to open it to find out more.

For example, something like "Inside: How to save 20% on your next service with us" is a simple yet effective way to drive curiosity and action.

4. Both Sides Matter

Don't forget the back of the envelope! People often focus on the front, but the back offers prime real estate for a message or graphic that can help reinforce your offer. It's another small touch that can make a big difference.

Back in the day, the *Readers Digest* used to go to great lengths to make their mailings look as if they'd been shipped by air mail. This trick made people receiving the mailers more likely to open them.

5. Consider Texture or Unusual Materials

While colour and size are effective, you can take it up a notch with texture. A textured or padded envelope or one printed on a heavier stock can give the impression of something premium inside. Or, for a really bold move, consider materials like vellum. This can create a talking point all on its own.

If you're targeting a high-end audience, this might be worth the investment. Imagine the impact of receiving an envelope that feels different in your hand. If it looks costly it sends a subliminal message: "This is important."

6. Personalisation

Finally, make sure your direct mail campaign feels personal. Addressing the envelope to the recipient by name, and possibly handwriting it, can significantly boost open rates. People are more likely to open something if they feel it's been sent specifically to them, rather than a generic mass mailer.

Envelopes: A Forgotten Opportunity?

The truth is, envelopes are often overlooked. But in today's world, where physical mail is a rarity, they represent an easy way to stand out from the crowd. And standing out is half the battle in marketing.

When was the last time you received something interesting in the post? Wouldn't it be nice if your business was the one that broke from routine and sent something memorable?

Take a lesson from my old college days – it's creativity and effort that turns something ordinary into something extraordinary. Whether it's colour, size, texture or a clever message, your envelope can be more than just packaging – it can become a key part of your marketing strategy.

If you're interested, my own student entry into the art school envelope challenge (as I'm now calling it) was an entirely see-through acrylic envelope. It certainly made an impression.

You're welcome to use that idea, especially if you want to highlight how transparent your pricing is.

See what I did there? I should get a job in marketing...

Key Takeaways

- Coloured envelopes grab attention and can reinforce your branding effectively.
- Unusual sizes or shapes, like tiny or oversized envelopes, create curiosity and stand out.
- Printing teaser messages on the front or back encourages recipients to open the mail.
- Textures or premium materials make envelopes feel special and hint at value inside.
- Personalised envelopes, especially with handwritten details, boost open rates.
- Physical mail is rare, so a creative envelope can make your business memorable.
- Envelopes are more than packaging – they can be a powerful marketing tool.

4

Postcards

> Postcards are a cost-effective and versatile tool for raising brand awareness and promoting products, services and events.

As I've mentioned before, the days of sorting through piles of junk mail are long gone. Nowadays, it's our email inboxes that are overflowing with promotional messages and newsletters. But that shift gives us an opportunity – physical mail, especially a humble postcard, now stands out like never before.

Postcards offer a unique advantage for businesses wanting to use the post as a means of communication. They're one of the most cost-effective ways to reach customers, combining a tangible, personal touch with the simplicity of a single, well-designed card. In a world dominated by digital marketing, this unusual approach can make your customers feel valued and considered.

Why Postcards?

First of all, if you're worried that sending postcards might make your business seem "down-market," let me reassure you – that's far from the case. Postcards can be designed to reflect the same professionalism and quality as any other marketing material. In fact, some of the world's most prestigious brands, like car manufacturers, use postcards for their customer communications.

And if it works for them, it can work for you too.

Postcards have several advantages:

- **Cost-Effectiveness**: They're inexpensive to print and send, making them an accessible option for businesses of any size.
- **Attention-Grabbing**: There's no envelope to open – your message is right there as soon as the recipient picks it up.
- **Memorability**: A well-designed postcard feels personal and, because it's a physical item, it's likely to be kept – maybe pinned to a board or displayed on a desk. Every time your customer sees it, they'll be reminded of your business.
- **Versatility**: You can use postcards for nearly any communication – special offers, event invites, thank you notes, reminders or simply staying in touch.

A Success Story

Let me share a little success story that illustrates the power of postcards. While working at an ad agency, I was involved in creating a series of after-sales postcards for Škoda. These weren't your average service reminders – they featured quirky, playful visuals that matched the brand's tone. The postcards reminded customers about upcoming MOTs, cambelt changes and brake checks. What was interesting is that these postcards were far more effective than their previous print reminders. The simple change in format caught people's attention and increased engagement.

The lesson here is that postcards don't have to be flashy or complicated – they just need to resonate with your audience.

Personal Touches Matter

One of the great things about postcards is that they allow you to add a personal touch without too much effort. When I send complimentary items like calendars to my clients, I include a handwritten note on a postcard I've bought cheaply from Amazon. But instead of using generic postcards, I choose reprints of vintage advertising cards relevant to my business. It's thoughtful, cost-effective, and leaves a lasting impression.

For instance, when I sent a gift to a book-writing coach, I enclosed a postcard featuring a 1950s Olivetti typewriter ad. It was a small, personal touch that made the communication more memorable.

You can do the same – find postcards that tie into your industry or reflect your brand's personality. A quick search on Amazon reveals plenty of options, from vintage travel posters to fashion, art and nature themed cards. Pick a set that resonates with your brand and use them to add an extra layer of thoughtfulness.

Practical Uses for Postcards in Your Business

So how can you use postcards effectively in your business?

- **Special Offers**: Send postcards to your existing customers with a time-limited offer or discount. Highlight the offer prominently so it grabs attention right away.
- **Event Invitations**: Invite customers to an event or launch using a beautifully designed postcard that reflects the theme or mood of the occasion.
- **Thank You Notes**: Send a personal thank you after a purchase or service. A simple message of appreciation goes a long way in building loyalty.
- **Appointment Reminders**: For service-based businesses, postcards make excellent appointment or service reminders. They're much harder to ignore than a digital notification.
- **Seasonal Greetings**: Use postcards to send holiday greetings or to mark special occasions. A festive postcard can put your business in a positive light and keep you in customers' minds.

Make Them Memorable

One of the key benefits of postcards is their staying power. If your postcard is attractive or creative, it's far less likely to be thrown away. In fact, your customers might display it in their workspace or on a pinboard, keeping your brand visible long after the initial contact.

To increase the chances of your postcard being kept, think about how you can add value or intrigue. Could you include a striking image, an inspiring quote or a clever design? And of course, don't forget to include your branding.

If your logo or brand message is visible on a card that stays in front of your customer for weeks, that's some powerful, long-term exposure.

Personalisation & Follow-Up

If you're sending postcards in bulk, try to personalise them as much as possible. Even small touches – like addressing the recipient by name – can make a huge difference. Personalisation helps your message feel less like a mass marketing attempt and more like a thoughtful gesture.

And don't forget to follow up! After sending out postcards, make sure to connect with your recipients. You can use a phone call, email or another piece of mail to reinforce your message and keep the conversation going.

The Elephant in the Post Room

Direct mail is unusual these days because marketing is digital-only for many businesses. But there is another reason for its seeming lack of popularity – the price of postage.

Digital printing costs have fallen tremendously over the last two decades, making printing letters and flyers cheaper than ever.

This cost-saving, however, is more than offset by the ever-rising price of a stamp. There are, however, some ways to reduce the cost of your mailings. These include:

Clean Up Your Mailing Lists

Your mailing lists are valuable tools in direct mail marketing. They include your target audience, as well as new and loyal customers.

Keeping your lists clean is crucial, because sending mail to the wrong address wastes money. Regularly remove duplicates, uninterested contacts or customers who have moved. This "list hygiene" ensures every mail piece reaches the right person, and you save money in the process.

Almost three-quarters of businesses that use direct mail clean their lists at least twice a year. Many mailing list companies update their data monthly to keep it current.

Segment your Lists

A direct mail campaign sent to the "right" people is more cost-effective. By not wasting money on people who don't want your mail, you can send fewer mailshots and get better results.

Segment your list to target the right audience and personalise your message to make it relevant.

Take Advantage of Bulk Postage Rates

There are several ways to save on bulk postage rates for your direct mail campaign:

- **Sort the Mail**: Pre-sorting the mail saves carriers time, so you get a discount on postage.
- **Use Mail Mark**: This service uses barcode technology to cut postage costs.
- **Advertising Mail Rates**: If your campaign is for advertising, you can get a lower postage rate than for business mail.

Remember you are not restricted to using only the Royal Mail – there are several other postal service providers, including UKMail, Citipost and Whistl.

Consider the Size and Shape of the Mailshot

The form of your mailshot matters. Unusual sizes, shapes or weights over a standard letter usually cost more to post. Plan your mailing to avoid these extra charges. For example, when I post out calendars to my clients, I ensure they will fit into a DL envelope, keeping the postage costs down.

Targeted Distribution: Avoid the Post Altogether

Another option for direct mail is to use targeted distribution services, otherwise known as EDDM (Every Door Direct Mail) or door drop marketing. These involve teams of people (private delivery companies or the Royal Mail) hand-delivering mailers in selected areas. The mail can be postcards, leaflets, flyers or brochures, and there is no need for envelopes, addresses or stamps.

Targeting can be achieved using a wide range of databases, but they will not be as accurate as if you were using your own list, and you cannot personalise the mailers. This makes targeted distribution more suitable for mass market campaigns when looking for new prospects in specific areas or certain types of property.

Services like this can include sophisticated tracking capabilities. Gone are the days when the delivery person could bin an entire batch of mailers and spend the afternoon in the pub with you none the wiser. Now, with GPS trackers, it's possible to monitor the delivery progress of your mailing down to street level in real-time.

Costs for this form of distribution are substantially cheaper than traditional postage. So much so that they can be coordinated with pay-per-click social media ad campaigns targeting the same delivery areas, and still be cheaper than a conventional direct mail campaign.

Key Takeaways

- Postcards stand out in today's digital-first world and are cost-effective to print and send.
- Their open format ensures your message is seen instantly without needing an envelope.
- A well-designed postcard feels personal and often gets kept, extending your brand's visibility.
- They're versatile – perfect for offers, invitations, reminders or thank you notes.
- Personalisation, like addressing recipients by name, makes them more impactful.
- Combining creativity with thoughtful design makes postcards memorable and effective.

5

Bookmarks

Bookmarks keep your brand in front of customers in a subtle way. They can boost brand awareness and customer retention while also reinforcing your reputation and encouraging engagement.

In the mid-90s, I studied marketing with the Chartered Institute of Marketing (CIM). Their diploma course was aimed at corporate marketing executives from the likes of Hasbro and Coca-Cola – not so much for lowly graphic designers like me at the time.

Ironically, as I absorbed corporate marketing theory, the internet arrived, and soon, many thought that everything we knew about marketing was going out of the window. Or so it seemed.

But when you look closely at today's digital marketing techniques, it's actually quite familiar. Take content marketing, for example. The premise is that you give away helpful content in exchange for potential customers' contact details, then nurture them towards a sale later on. It feels revolutionary, but it's not new.

In fact, content marketing is a modern twist on the direct response marketing tactics of the 1890s. John Deere, the US tractor manufacturer, began sending out free newsletters to its customers in 1895, and that is now considered to be one of the first examples of content marketing.

Back then, advertisers relied on newspaper ads with coupons offering free samples. Today, we use blogs, videos and social media posts to entice people with free downloads. The media has changed, but the mechanics haven't.

The principles of content marketing – offering value first to build trust – are reflected in a much more traditional, yet still powerful, tool: bookmarks. They provide something useful while quietly keeping your brand in your customers' minds.

Why Bookmarks Work as a Marketing Tool

Bookmarks are simple, practical, and most importantly, long-lasting. As a physical object, a bookmark doesn't get tossed aside or forgotten like many digital promotions. It stays with the reader, offering repeated brand exposure every time they use it.

If your business has any connection to publishing or writing, or even if your target audience is a "bookish" crowd, creating your own branded bookmarks is a no-brainer. And even if your business doesn't directly connect to books, bookmarks can still be a great tool – creative, easy to distribute and budget-friendly.

Creative Uses for Bookmarks

Bookmarks offer endless opportunities for businesses to get creative. For instance, if your business sells physical products, consider adding a branded bookmark as a thoughtful bonus with every order. It's a simple, low-cost way to show attention to detail, and it's practical for your customers. Bookstores, of course, are the perfect fit for this, but even unrelated businesses can use bookmarks to offer something useful that feels like a little gift.

You can use bookmarks as a promotional tool by turning them into mini flyers. Include special offers, discount codes or loyalty systems right on the bookmark itself. Something as simple as "Use this code for 10% off your next purchase" can add significant value. You can even create referral opportunities by encouraging customers to pass your bookmark along to a friend, giving both the referrer and the new customer a special discount in return. This way, your bookmarks work to multiply their impact.

Bookmarks can also reflect your brand story. If sustainability is a key part of your brand, why not print your bookmarks on FSC-certified paper and use the space to share your eco-friendly mission? Or, if you're a service-based business, you could add motivational quotes, tips or industry-related facts that resonate with your audience. These little touches turn a practical item into something that reinforces your message.

Another idea is to make your bookmarks interactive. Adding a QR code that links to exclusive content, a helpful guide or even a promotional video can add another layer of engagement. This turns a traditional bookmark into a bridge between physical and digital marketing, offering more value to your customers while guiding them back to your online space.

For businesses attending events, bookmarks make for ideal handouts. Whether it's a trade show, local networking or a seminar, bookmarks are a lightweight, practical giveaway. Plus, they offer more space to communicate your message while maintaining that personal touch.

Seasonal campaigns are another way to make the most of bookmarks. You can create limited edition designs for holidays or special occasions, making your marketing feel timely and relevant. Whether it's a Christmas-themed bookmark or something for Halloween, these seasonal touches add novelty and make your brand stand out.

An unusual creative approach is to design bookmarks that can be coloured in. Known as mindfulness colouring bookmarks, these are great for children's wellbeing, been proven to reduce anxiety.

And if you want to spend a little bit more for something unique, why not die-cut the tops of your bookmarks so the part that sticks out of the pages is a quirky shape? You could have some real fun creating something that relates to your business in an unusual way.

Practical Benefits of Bookmarks

- **Great Value**: Bookmarks can be incredibly cheap to produce, especially in bulk, making them a cost-effective marketing tool that fits within even the tightest budgets.
- **Long-Lasting**: Because bookmarks are used repeatedly, they have a long shelf life. Each time a customer opens their book, they'll see your brand, reinforcing their connection with your business.
- **Highly Customisable**: A bookmark may be small, but it offers plenty of room for creativity. Think of it as a miniature flyer for your business.
- **Easy to Distribute**: Lightweight and portable, bookmarks are easy to hand out at events, send with orders or include in mailings. They're cheap to send and easy to include in business correspondence.

- **Perfect for Niche Markets:** If your business relates to education, publishing or the arts, bookmarks are a natural fit. But even if it doesn't, their practicality and design potential make them a versatile marketing tool.
- **Encourage Repeat Business:** By adding a special offer, discount code or loyalty stamp system to your bookmark, you can incentivise customers to return.
- **Feels Like a Gift:** Unlike a flyer or brochure, a well-designed bookmark feels more like a gift than an ad. This adds a personal touch, which can lead to a more positive impression of your brand.

Consider the Design

Design matters when it comes to bookmarks. Think about how you can use your design to tell a story or highlight a key message. Is there a particular product or service you want to promote? Do you have a slogan that sums up your brand's mission? Include that on your bookmark.

Any print finishing technique that can be applied to business cards can also be added to bookmarks. So if spot varnish, matt or velvet lamination, foil blocking or embossing suit your brand, consider adding them to your bookmarks.

Lastly, don't forget that good design makes things memorable. A beautifully designed bookmark is far more likely to be kept and used over and over again.

Key Takeaways

- Bookmarks are practical, long-lasting and keep your brand visible every time they're used.
- They're cost-effective to produce and feel like a thoughtful gift rather than a sales pitch.
- Adding offers, discount codes or loyalty elements can encourage repeat business.
- Custom designs, including seasonal themes or interactive QR codes, will enhance their appeal.
- Lightweight and portable, bookmarks are easy to hand out to customers or include with orders.

6

Pens

> Pens are practical and highly visible, making them perfect for generating brand awareness.

As I sit at my desk, it's hard not to notice the sea of promotional stuff around me. A loyalty card here, a desk calendar there... and, of course, the ultimate marketing ninja – the branded pen. Unlike most of the throwaway promo junk that ends up in landfill, a well-made pen can stay in someone's hand (or pocket) for years. And that's where your brand can literally make its mark.

While some promotional items are quickly forgotten, lost or thrown away, a good pen has staying power. Think about it – when was the last time you threw away a pen? Chances are, it's still in your drawer or your bag, doing exactly what it should – keeping someone's brand in front of its customers for the long haul.

I'm sure we've all experienced grabbing a complimentary pen, maybe some months ago at a random event, and found it still going strong and somehow never leaving your desk. Now imagine that pen had your brand on it – how many times would your business get noticed?

Quality Signalling

If you promote your business with a premium pen, it has a weight to it – the smooth glide of ink on paper, the satisfying click of the cap, that moment when you realise this isn't just a pen, it's your pen. And if it's got your brand on it, that's exactly the kind of experience you want to be giving your customers.

Conversely, a budget, poorly made pen that falls apart within days and doesn't write properly will only cheapen your brand.

Branded promotional pens are practical, cost-effective and widely used. Here's why they might be a smart choice for your business:

- **Popular**: Whether at work, school or home, pens are something everyone uses. When you give out a branded pen, it's likely to be used regularly. This means your business name or logo will be seen repeatedly, boosting your brand recognition.
- **Long-Lasting**: Unlike many other promotional items, pens tend to have a long life. There's a pen in my collection promoting Windows 95 – it outlasted the software it was advertising by over 20 years! This extended use ensures that your brand stays in the hands of customers for a long time.
- **Versatile**: Promotional pens are suitable for a wide range of settings. Hand them out at trade shows, conferences or community events. You can include them in welcome packs, giveaways or as a token of appreciation to loyal customers. Their versatility makes them a superb marketing tool.

Options Galore

When you're considering branded pens, there are thousands to choose from at all price levels.

If you're feeling fancy, there's the Waterman® Expert – your business name engaved on the barrel, giving off serious "I mean business" vibes, and a snip at £75 each. On the other hand, if you're not looking to break the bank, there are budget ballpoints on the market at 17p per unit... just remember, you get what you pay for, and no one wants their brand associated with a pen that dies mid-signature.

If you offer a quality service, you shouldn't spoil it with a cheap and nasty complimentary pen.

Eco-friendly pens made from recycled or sustainable materials show your commitment to the environment and will appeal to eco-conscious customers – a simple, effective way to promote your business while supporting sustainability.

Bear in mind when ordering pens that there is usually a minimum order quantity, which is sometimes quite substantial. A few years ago, I fell in love with a really nice pen made from 100% recycled plastic. It wrote smoothly, it felt comfortable in my hand as I was writing and they could be ordered to exactly match my brand colour.

When I enquired about buying some for myself the minimum order was 500. I don't know that many people and, had I ordered them, I'd still probably have 400 left! And as I changed my logo a year later, it was just as well I didn't order them.

Pens of All Types for All Professions

The breadth of options available is impressive, too, and you don't need to confine yourself to ballpoint pens. For example, if you are in education, why not give away your own branded highlighters?

There are pens with antimicrobial coatings – great for medical businesses, and pens with torches in them – ideal for someone, I'm sure. Maybe cinema usherettes or coal miners.

There are pens with multiple ink colours and others with rubber styluses that you can use on a smartphone instead of your finger (useful if your customer's job requires wearing gloves).

If you steer slightly more into the novelty selections, you can find promotional pens that look like lipstick, syringes, darts or pens that double as bookmarks. The Windows 95 pen I have is a banner pen – it features a pull-out double-sided graphic that rolls around the inner barrel of the pen.

Whichever you choose the goal is the same – keeping your brand in your customers' hands.

Don't Forget Pencils

One of the nicest looking promo pens I have is actually a propelling pencil. And if you have a horticultural or eco-friendly element to your business, **Sprout** are a Danish company who produce plantable pencils that feature a seed pod in a cellulose cap at the end. Once you are finished using your pencil, you can plant it in a pot and eventually it will grow into flowers or herbs.

The branding element to these is interesting - you can have your business name on the pencil itself, but they also sell customisable packaging for the pencils, as sleeves, boxes and even a notebook. These would make great promotional items for product launches, trade shows and conferences, campaigns or as client gifts. Check them out at *sproutworld.com*.

So, next time you're looking for a way to keep your brand in people's hands, consider a simple, effective tool that they'll actually want to hold onto - your very own branded pen.

Key Takeaways

- Branded pens are practical, widely used and keep your brand visible for a long time.
- A high-quality pen reflects well on your business, while cheap ones can harm your image.
- Pens are versatile - perfect for trade shows, giveaways or as tokens of appreciation.
- Eco-friendly pens show your commitment to sustainability and appeal to eco-conscious buyers.
- There's a huge range of pens available at widely-ranging price points.
- Novelty options like banner pens or plantable pencils can add creativity and increase engagement.
- Check minimum order quantities as they can sometimes be substantial.
- A good pen feels like a gift, leaving a positive and lasting impression of your business.

7

Drinkware

> Branded drinkware gives your customers a daily reminder of your brand, helping with awareness and customer retention.

While researching this book, I've probed the weirdest and most obscure corners of the internet for your benefit, and for this chapter, I happened upon an interesting-sounding Australian article called **Mugs: 20 Fascinating Facts**.

Some of the "facts" contained therein could be better described as padding, and that's being generous. For example, brace yourself for Fact No.5: *In the United Kingdom, mugs are sometimes referred to as "cups" or "tea cups."*

Take that, fact fans! You can bank that one for your next pub quiz.

But the article gets back on track with the claim that the world's oldest promotional mug dates back to 1865, when a potter named Thomas Briar created a mug with the name "George" on it.

Who the mysterious George was, and whether this fact is even true, I have no idea. But T. Briar, Esq., was on to something, because the promotional products market in the UK is now worth over £1 billion a year.

As I mentioned in the previous section, there are lots of wasteful promotional products that I'm not too keen on. But the more useful it is, the more I like it.

One thing I rely on heavily in my office is coffee, and I drink plenty of it from my own branded coffee mug.

I initially ordered personalised mugs for my business during the COVID lockdown, where we had no alternative but to endure endless Zoom-based business meetings.

It seemed like an ideal chance to display some on-screen branding while simultaneously enjoying more coffee!

Promotional mugs can make perfect business giveaways. They work equally well in creating brand awareness as they do in publicising new products, services or campaigns.

And they last practically forever.

I worked with a guy a few years ago who would only drink tea from a branded Aston Villa FC mug that was at least 20 years old.

The interior of that mug was in such a revolting condition that no one else would go anywhere near it. Two decades of builder's brew had turned it into something a scientist could study in a search for new life.

But it's also a great example of brand loyalty and the longevity of the promotional mug.

There is plenty of choice – you don't have to confine yourself to standard coffee mugs. These days, you can personalise espresso sets, porcelain teacups, bone china mugs and even those extra-large buckets-o-tea they have at Sports Direct.

And moving away from coffee, water bottles are also a prime candidate for branding. If your business is related to fitness and health, branded drinks bottles for the gym would be a great choice. Think about the type of customer you have and what would work for them.

Here are some reasons why branded drinkware could be a great addition to your promotional strategy:

- **Daily Visibility**: Coffee mugs and drinks containers are items people use every day, whether at home, in the office or on the go. Every time someone reaches for their morning coffee or their water bottle, your brand gets noticed.
- **Long-Lasting**: As we've seen with the 20-year-old Aston Villa mug, drinks containers are built to last. A well-made mug or bottle can last for years, and this longevity ensures that your brand remains in circulation for a long time, providing ongoing advertising at no extra cost.
- **Practical**: Everyone needs a mug for their tea or coffee and a container for water or other drinks. These items are not just promotional gimmicks

– they are genuinely useful. When you give customers something they can use every day, they are more likely to appreciate it and remember you.

- **Customisable**: Coffee mugs and drinks containers offer a large area for branding. You can include your logo and tagline, a fun design, or even a photo or message. This flexibility gives you the scope to create a giveaway that not only promotes your business but also looks appealing and professional.

Eco-Friendly Options

There are over 2.5 billion single-use coffee cups thrown away each year in the UK. With increasing awareness of environmental issues, many people prefer reusable drinks containers over disposable ones, and many coffee chains now offer a discount if you bring in your own.

Eco-friendly options include stainless steel mugs and mugs made from 100% recycled plastic. Using branded sustainable drinks containers can enhance your brand image and attract customers who care about sustainability.

Branded promotional coffee mugs and drinks containers are an effective marketing tool for small businesses. They provide daily, long-lasting visibility, are practical and useful, and offer great customisation options. They are portable, versatile and can enhance your brand image, particularly if you choose eco-friendly options.

Branded mugs – subtle marketing, one sip at a time.

With advances in printing techniques, there is often no minimum order quantity – so you can order singles if necessary.

As a final idea, when you give them to customers, why not add a quality teabag or a coffee sachet and some biscuits, with a note saying, "Let's meet up for a brew"?

Who could possibly refuse such a thoughtful offer?

(And if you wanted to push the boat out even further, why not give away matching branded coasters?)

Key Takeaways

- Branded drinkware like mugs and water bottles provides daily visibility for your brand.
- These items are practical, long-lasting, and stay in use for years, offering ongoing exposure.
- Customisation options allow for creative branding that feels professional and appealing.
- Eco-friendly drinkware appeals to environmentally conscious customers and enhances your image.
- Combining coffee mugs with extras, like a teabag, coffee sachet or branded coaster, can make your giveaway more memorable.
- Advances in printing mean you can often order in small quantities, keeping costs manageable.

8

Loyalty Cards

> Loyalty cards reward repeat customers, boosting retention and sales. They're also effective for encouraging cross-selling, upselling and engagement through special offers.

For any small business, particularly those in retail, retaining customers is crucial for success. One effective way to drive repeat business is by offering printed loyalty cards. These little cards not only bring customers back but also serve as a powerful and cost-effective marketing tool.

As I mentioned in the intro to this section, I was a happy, loyal customer of the Caffé Nero coffee chain for a few years while I worked in Nottingham. This loyalty was partly due to personal preference – Costa always seems soulless, and Starbucks coffee tastes like mud.

Which reminds me of one of my favourite Dad jokes:

Man: Waiter, this coffee tastes like mud!

Waiter: That is because it was ground half an hour ago, sir.

Ahem, anyway... I kept returning to Caffé Nero because of their simple loyalty card scheme. Get ten stamps, and your next coffee was free. And each time I came back, I didn't just buy coffee, but a sandwich and some crisps too. Good business for them.

Sadly, for me (and Caffé Nero's shareholders), I now work from home, and there isn't a branch within 20 miles of where I live. But whenever I visit a city and fancy a coffee, I will hunt out a Caffé Nero first, because loyalty lasts.

Why Customer Loyalty Matters

Loyal customers generate repeat sales and promote your business to others. Focusing on loyalty helps SMEs to create a solid customer base, providing stability and growth.

By offering incentives and rewards to loyal customers, you strengthen their connection to your brand, which encourages them to choose your business over your competitor down the road.

Loyal customers can also provide you with valuable feedback and insights, helping you to improve your products or services. This direct communication is crucial for innovation and staying ahead in the market.

Additionally, loyal customers are less price-sensitive. They will pay more for products or services if they trust your brand, which ultimately results in higher profit margins for you.

Implementing a Reward System

An effective reward system encourages customers to participate in your loyalty programme. You can offer incentives that appeal to your target audience and align with your business goals.

These incentives could be discounts on future purchases, exclusive access to promotions or free gifts. By tailoring the rewards to your customers' needs, you'll make your programme more appealing.

You could design tiered rewards to recognise different levels of loyalty. Offer basic incentives for new customers and exclusive perks for those who are long-term or high spenders. This approach motivates customers to progress through the tiers, creating a sense of achievement.

Designing Eye-Catching Loyalty Cards

Your cards should obviously reflect your brand and attract attention.

Consider hiring a professional designer to create a visually appealing card. Ensure the design matches your brand's colours and prominently features your logo. Don't forget to include contact information and any terms and conditions.

When printing, use uncoated card stock if you're using a stamp to avoid smudging. If yours is a more premium business, a glossy finish can give a premium look for more sophisticated loyalty cards. You could even explore embossing or foil stamping for added luxury.

Adding unique elements like QR codes or scratch-off panels can also make your loyalty cards stand out. These features can increase engagement and make your programme more memorable.

Integrating Technology

If you're tech-savvy, technology can enhance modern loyalty programmes, allowing you to gather valuable data on customer behaviour and preferences by using QR codes and barcodes.

Scanning these codes at the point-of-sale allows you to track which products or services customers redeem their rewards for. This can help you to identify trends, optimise your offerings and tailor your future promotions.

As well as for tracking purchases, QR codes can link to extra content or digital promotions on your website. Alternatively, they can direct customers to online satisfaction surveys, personalised offers, mailing list sign-up forms or your social media profiles to engage them further.

Strategies for Distributing Loyalty Cards

Train your staff to naturally introduce your loyalty programme and offer cards to every customer. Encouraging word-of-mouth can be as simple as giving out a few extra cards for customers to share with friends and family. Including loyalty cards with purchases is a thoughtful touch and exploring partnerships with local businesses or events that attract your target audience is another way to enhance your programme's reach.

A Step-by-Step Guide to Setting Up a Loyalty Card Programme

Setting up a printed loyalty card scheme might sound daunting, but it's actually quite straightforward. Here's a simple step-by-step guide to get you started:

1. **Begin with Clear Goals**
Before anything else, decide what you want your loyalty programme to achieve. Are you aiming to boost customer visits, increase average spend or simply build a stronger relationship with your clientele? Clear goals will help you shape the rest of your programme.

2. **Design with Purpose**
A well-designed loyalty card should be both functional and visually appealing. Consider how your brand's identity will be reflected in the card. Remember to leave space for those all-important stamps and any terms and conditions that customers need to know.

3. **Decide on the Reward Structure**
Think about what will entice your customers to keep coming back. A common approach is to offer a free item or a discount after a certain number of purchases. Keep it simple – for example, "Buy 10, Get 1 Free." This straightforward approach is easy for both your customers and your staff to understand and manage.

4. **Order Your Supplies**
You'll need printed cards and a custom stamp. Both are affordable and easy to order online or through a local print shop. Make sure the stamp design is clear and consistent, as this will be the mark of your loyalty scheme. Ensure you have plenty of stamps and cards on hand, especially if you're running a high-traffic business.

5. **Train Your Staff**
Ensure your staff are familiar with the loyalty programme and encourage them to offer cards to every customer. A quick, friendly explanation of the rewards goes a long way in getting customers on board. You could even make it a part of your regular customer interaction, like handing a card with each purchase.

6. **Launch and Promote Your Programme**
Once everything is in place, it's time to launch. Spread the word about your new loyalty programme – display information in your shop, mention it on social media and encourage staff to talk about it. You might even consider offering an initial bonus, like double stamps for the first week, to get things rolling and generate initial excitement.

7. Monitor and Adjust

Once your loyalty programme is up and running, keep an eye on its performance. Are customers engaging with it? Is it creating repeat business? Don't be afraid to tweak the reward structure or promotion strategy based on what you observe.

Caffé Nero eventually abandoned their simple card-based loyalty system in favour of a smartphone app. While the rewards were the same, using the app left me feeling disconnected.

Part of the joy of the old loyalty card experience was the human interaction of talking to the barista, handing over your card, having them stamp it and getting it back.

Occasionally, if the barista felt generous, or if you smiled at them nicely and asked for an extra shot in your Americano, you'd sometimes get two stamps (don't tell the boss).

This simple interaction doesn't sound like much, but using the replacement app was much less satisfying once the purchasing experience was reduced to the "bip" of scanning in a QR code from your phone.

And you never got double stamps, either.

Stay Inspired

Stay inspired and keep your marketing fresh! Sign up for the *20 Ways* mailing list to get exclusive tips, updates and resources to help your business stand out using print and beyond. It's free and easy to join, I promise to never sell your data, and you can leave at any time. Come and join us!

Key Takeaways

- Loyalty cards are a simple, cost-effective way to encourage repeat retail business and strengthen customer relationships.
- Clear, enticing rewards like "Buy 10, Get 1 Free" make loyalty programmes easy to understand and appealing.
- A professionally designed card that reflects your brand adds credibility and encourages engagement.
- Offering unique touches like QR codes or scratch-off panels can make your cards stand out and feel more interactive.
- Train staff to introduce the programme naturally and provide cards with purchases to maximise uptake.
- Distributing extra cards for customers to share can spread word-of-mouth and expand your reach.
- Monitoring and adjusting your programme ensures it remains effective and engaging over time.
- Printed loyalty cards create a personal connection with customers that smartphone apps often fail to replicate.

9

Stickers

> Stickers are fun and eye-catching, perfect for spreading brand awareness and driving social media engagement. They're also handy for promoting events and sparking customer interest.

As a young oik in the 1970s, I used to collect Topps chewing gum Wanted stickers. I've just looked on eBay, and someone is selling a complete set of 1975 originals for $250 – so they have certainly appreciated as an investment.

Sadly, I stuck mine to various surfaces – books, doors, the cat – thus rendering them unfit for resale purposes. Another money-making opportunity down the drain!

You might think of stickers primarily as something you'd use to keep children entertained. But in the world of small business marketing, they're super-versatile.

Aside from the obvious use of stickers for addressing envelopes, stickers can also help you to bring out your creative side. They don't have to be serious or boring – in fact they are a great way to add a touch of humour or a quirky message if it fits your brand's personality.

For example, a letter with a colourful sticker that hints at what's inside will create a sense of anticipation and make people more likely to open it.

Stickers can also be included inside direct mail pieces. Mail a special offer or discount code on a sticker that customers can peel off and keep. It's a great way to make sure your message sticks around (literally) instead of being thrown away with the rest of the post.

These are just a few examples of creative ways stickers can help you in your marketing. But there are also good business and marketing considerations why sticker marketing (which is a thing, apparently) should be a part of your promotional toolkit.

A Small But Mighty Marketing Tool

You might not immediately think that using stickers makes good business sense, but here are some points to consider.

- **Cost-effective**: Stickers offer a highly affordable way to enhance your brand visibility at low cost. Adding them to envelopes or product packaging is significantly cheaper than printing directly on the envelopes or packaging boxes themselves. This makes them ideal for businesses looking to maximise their brand impact on a budget.
- **Versatile**: Stickers can be used across a wide range of marketing platforms, from packaging and street marketing to digital integration via QR codes, which makes them highly adaptable.

Marketing Considerations

- **Community Building**: Stickers can help create a sense of community and belonging among your customers, creating stronger emotional ties to your brand.

  Apple, who get lauded for all manner of highly sophisticated marketing tactics, have given away loose stickers inside their product packaging for over 25 years. Giving their buyers a shiny Apple logo sticker with their high-tech computer or phone probably costs Apple fractions of cents – but they wouldn't do it if there was no brand value to it. (I stuck the first one I ever received to our office wastebasket – it seemed amusing at the time.)

  Fashion brands, including sportswear, footwear and children's clothes, make great use of stickers as giveaways to further their brand awareness and visibility.
- **Audience Engagement**: Stickers are a great way to boost interaction with your customers. They can encourage social media sharing, create excitement through contests, or simply be added to personal items like laptops,

notebooks or water bottles. Consider including stickers in a loyalty program or as a thank you gift with purchases. When customers display them, they're effectively providing free advertising for your business.

- **Tracking and digital interaction**: You can make your stickers more functional by incorporating QR codes or other digital elements, linking them with digital marketing campaigns, your social media and your website. Unique QR codes can also be used to track website visits, so you can monitor how successful a sticker campaign is and how long your stickers last.

  Share photos of your stickers in action on social media, and if you include a unique hashtag you can encourage your followers to do the same. You can even turn this into a competition to create more noise around your business.

Guerrilla Marketing

Guerrilla marketing is a strategy that uses unconventional, low-cost tactics to promote a product, service or brand. The aim is to spark interest and create a buzz through creative, unexpected approaches that reach a wide audience, all without relying on expensive traditional advertising.

Using stickers in unconventional ways, such as street level marketing, is a perfect example of guerrilla marketing. With stickers you can generate excitement, provoke curiosity and spread the word about your business, possibly even leading to viral social media exposure.

Stickers have been used for decades by music fans and football supporters, leaving their tribal signs stuck to lampposts, toilet cisterns, train carriages, pubs and anywhere else they can find.

One of my sons takes great delight in rediscovering his old high school rock band stickers in pubs across the East Midlands – these stickers have been there, undisturbed by cleaning staff for at least 12 years. (Not sure what that says about the hygiene of the pubs of Leicester, Derby and Nottingham, but there you go.)

Guerrilla marketing with stickers won't work for every business – but you never know. Sometimes the best ideas emerge when you combine two seemingly unrelated concepts. For example, if your business offers something people look forward to (like holidays, spa treatments or premium food and drink), you could place advertising stickers in places they'd rather avoid (like a crowded commuter train). This could form the foundation of a guerrilla sticker campaign, whether for local exposure or to spark broader interest. Give it a go and see where it leads (but read the upcoming legal and ethical discussion first).

Thinking Bigger

Stickers also have a role to play in point-of-sale displays and retail environments. Window and floor stickers can attract attention to promotions and new stock. In my design agency days, we produced floor stickers in the shape of cartoon monster footprints for Škoda showrooms when they launched their Yeti model. And during the pandemic, floor stickers appeared everywhere, reminding people in the UK what a two-metre queuing distance looked like.

And finally, why not bring back the car bumper sticker. They were hugely popular when I was a kid, but you rarely see car stickers anymore. See if you can come up with something better than "My other car is a Porsche".

Practical Considerations

Finally, some notes on the practicalities of sticker marketing.

Design and Branding

Consistency is key in all marketing, and stickers are no exception. Remain consistent to your brand's identity by using the same logos, colours and messaging. This way, when people see your stickers, they'll immediately recognise your brand, making it easier for them to remember you and what you have to offer.

When designing anything, the smaller the space, the more important it is to get the basics right. When the print area is at a premium, less is definitely more. Prioritise quality over quantity by honing in on your core brand elements. Do you need a web address and phone number, or would a QR code be better? Stickers are also not the place for bullet point lists of features.

Whatever you do, make sure your design is legible at its finished size. Print it out and try to read it yourself. A common mistake is assuming that, just because it's clear on screen, it will be equally clear at its printed dimensions.

Try to avoid the mistake of printing QR code stickers on a low-quality home inkjet printer. It's all too easy to launch your campaign, only to discover that the stickers are too small and blurry for cameras to scan properly (I've seen it happen more than once).

Materials

Stickers should be high quality to withstand different conditions, like outdoor exposure, so they stay effective over time without fading or deteriorating.

So, choose your materials with care, considering how and where the stickers will be used. For example, do they need to resist UV light, be waterproof or require strong adhesive, or conversely do they need to be removeable? Should you need to, you can protect and lengthen the life of your stickers by having them laminated.

Remember that you are not confined to printing only on paper – transparent polypropylene or vinyl stickers make great additions to windows or clear bottles. Environmentally friendly materials, including recycled paper, and those made from grass pulp, can help you to reinforce an eco-conscious brand message.

And if you're producing stickers or self-adhesive labels for food packaging, you have a wide range of specialist materials to choose from. Ask your printer for more advice.

Legal and Ethical Issues

When it comes to marketing your business, there is always some form of meddling bureaucracy lurking in the background, with the sole aim of hampering progress and the way to wealth. Attaching a few harmless stickers to public spaces is one of those totally legitimate aspects of commerce that is frowned upon by people like these, who you'd think would have more important things to worry about.

On a more serious note, you can't just plaster your web address on every bus shelter in town and expect to avoid legal letters and a cleaning bill from your local bus company.

While guerrilla sticker marketing can be an eye-catching way to promote your brand, it's important to tread carefully to avoid crossing the line into vandalism or property damage. Placing stickers on private property without permission could result in fines or legal action, as well as upset to property owners.

Public spaces bring their own challenges, with laws and regulations differing between councils and regions, so you'll need to research and follow the rules to steer clear of unwanted trouble. Many local authorities would regard stickering in the same way as they do flyposting – illegal.

Finally, the choice of location is critical because inappropriate or offensive placement could harm your brand's reputation and send the wrong message about your values.

Stick With It

Stickers might be small, but they can have a big impact on your marketing efforts. Whether you're using them for packaging, labelling, direct mail, giveaways or even on the street, they're a versatile and cost-effective way to promote your brand.

If you want to stick in your customers' minds, use a sticker.

Key Takeaways

- Stickers are versatile, cost-effective, and can add a creative touch to your marketing efforts.
- They can enhance packaging, direct mail and giveaways while remaining budget-friendly.
- Adding QR codes or discount offers makes stickers interactive and can boost customer engagement.
- High-quality materials ensure stickers last, whether on packaging, windows or outdoor surfaces.
- Consistent branding on stickers reinforces recognition and builds trust with your audience.
- Guerrilla marketing with stickers in unexpected places can create buzz and attract attention.
- Stickers can used to build a sense of community and loyalty when part of a larger campaign.

Intermission

D.I.Why?

When small business owners think about design, one name often comes up: Canva. It's the go-to platform for creating quick and easy creative layouts, especially for those on a budget.

Canva markets itself as a simple solution for non-designers, giving everyone the ability to create logos, flyers and social media graphics with just a few clicks. But, as appealing as it sounds, there's a deeper issue – a trade-off between the convenience of doing it yourself and the value that professional design can give to your business.

Let's imagine for a moment that you've decided to take on graphic design as a new career path. You could enrol in a university programme, spend years learning the nuances of typography, colour theory and software like Adobe Illustrator, Photoshop, InDesign and Figma. Alternatively, you could dive straight into on-the-job training, gaining hands-on experience with printing and real-world client projects.

Either way, the journey to becoming a skilled designer is long, requiring both creative talent and extensive technical know-how.

But who needs all that training and experience when you have Canva? It's quick, cheap and accessible, making design seem like something anyone can do. However, the convenience comes with hidden costs, especially when it comes to print marketing, where Canva's weaknesses become glaringly obvious.

The Hidden Costs of DIY Design

The first thing to understand is that Canva was never designed for print. While it's great for digital graphics like social media posts, it falls short when producing physical marketing materials such as flyers or brochures.

Canva operates in the RGB colour space used by computer screens, whereas print requires a different space, CMYK, which leads to colour conversion issues that users may not notice until it's too late. Even for those aware of the difference, Canva lacks the tools needed to manage these transitions effectively, making it difficult to achieve professional results. Although the Pro version lets you export a PDF in CMYK mode, this happens at the end of the design process with no control over the conversion – unlike in professional design software, where you can work in CMYK from the start.

Why is this important? A common example is when designing using a photograph with a vibrant blue sky. It looks stunning on screen (RGB) but appears muddy and dull in print (CMYK) because the RGB colour space is larger – certain colours that you can see on screen simply can't be converted accurately. (If you ever find yourself unable to sleep, Google "colour management" – five minutes in, you'll be well on the way to a full night's blissful rest.)

Beyond colour, there are a host of other technical issues to consider in print design – image resolution, bleed, trapping, font licensing, PDF output intent and many more. These are terms most Canva users will never have heard of, but they are all crucial to ensuring design is printed correcly. Professional designers spend years mastering these intricacies to ensure that what looks good on screen also looks great on paper. Canva, with its templates and drag-and-drop simplicity, glosses over these details, leaving many small business owners with marketing materials that don't print well and fail to make a good impression.

Design isn't just about making things look pretty. Its primary job is communication – conveying your brand's message clearly and effectively. A professionally designed logo or marketing piece is more than just a collection of shapes and colours – the design reflects your business's values and identity.

By using a generic Canva template, however, you run a high risk of blending in with the thousands of other businesses using the same tools. You might think your DIY design is unique, but a quick reverse image search in Google Images can often reveal that hundreds of others are using the exact same template, only with different names slapped on.

Cognitive Biases and the Canva Trap

So aside from cost, why do so many people buy into Canva's promises? The answer lies in its clever use of two powerful cognitive biases - mental shortcuts that shape how we all perceive our skills and creations. These two are the Dunning-Kruger Effect and the IKEA Effect.

The Dunning-Kruger Effect can lead people to overestimate their abilities. Often mentioned in relation to politicians who seem underqualified, this bias also plays out in Canva's user-friendly interface, which allows anyone to produce something that looks half-decent. However, this ease of use can create a false impression of the user's design abilities.

Because Canva users can quickly assemble a flyer or social media graphic, they may assume that professional design must be simple - and not worth the investment.

Then there's the IKEA Effect, which causes people to overvalue things they've made themselves. Just as building flat-pack furniture gives an unearned sense of pride, creating a design in Canva can lead to an emotional attachment to it. Even if the design has clear flaws, this sense of ownership can make it hard to recognise them.

Unfortunately, this often results in shoddy printed marketing that doesn't hit the mark and fails to communicate effectively.

The Real-World Consequences of Canva-Generated Print

While Canva works for quick, digital graphics, print is a different ball game. In my experience, the hallmarks of a Canva-generated print piece include blurry, low-resolution images, unsuitable typefaces, illegible text that's often too close to the edge of the sheet, and stock photos you've seen a thousand times before.

As someone who's worked in design for decades, I've seen countless examples of client-made print designs (using totally inappropriate tools like Canva, but also Word, Powerpoint – even Excel) that fail to meet even the most basic professional standards. These designs often lack crucial elements like a clear call to action, readable fonts or consideration for folds or trimmed edges.

In the end, poor design hurts your business. When your marketing materials look amateurish, potential customers will assume the same about your services. They might not consciously notice every flaw, but their overall perception of your brand will be shaped by the quality of your materials.

And when those materials look cheap, your business looks cheap too.

The False Promise of Templates

Templates are Canva's bread and butter, offering a quick solution for businesses that don't have the budget for custom design. But while templates might save time, they come with significant downsides.

By their very nature, templates are generic. They're designed to appeal to a broad audience, which means they will never capture the unique essence of your brand.

When you use a Canva template, you're effectively squeezing your business into a pre-made mould, one that hundreds, if not thousands, of other businesses are already using. You might think you're saving money, but what you're really doing is undermining your brand's uniqueness.

Moreover, templates encourage complacency. It's easy to settle for "good enough" when the template does most of the work for you. But standing out in a crowded market requires more than just filling in the blanks. It takes creativity, innovation and a clear understanding of your brand's voice and values – things that Canva's templates can never fully provide.

Canva's Popularity vs. Professional Design

Let's be honest: Canva's popularity stems mostly from the fact that it's cheap and easy. For a small business owner with limited resources, Canva seems like a no-brainer. But what people forget is that money spent on design is really an investment in your business, not a cost.

Good design can generate leads, boost sales and build long-term brand loyalty. When you think of design as an investment, the equation changes. It's not about saving a few pounds today – it's about setting your business up for success tomorrow.

As a business owner, your time is incredibly precious. As Tony Tran from fintech services provider Lumanu puts it, "Time is so much more valuable when you're a small business than when you're a big company." The decision to save money by doing it yourself comes at the cost of your time – the most valuable asset you have as a small business owner.

When you spend time on important but non-core tasks, like accounting or design, you're not able to focus on growing your business. What's the cost of missing out on new clients or business development opportunities because you're bogged down with bookkeeping or Canva?

Outsourcing isn't about *not being able* to do it yourself. It's about being *strategic* with your time and resources. By focusing on what you do best and letting experts handle the rest, you're setting your business up for long-term success. Outsourcing design to a professional is a win-win – it frees up your time and ensures that your brand looks polished, consistent and credible.

Design as a Long-Term Investment

Investing in design for your business brings both immediate and long-term rewards. In the short term, good design helps you grab attention in a competitive landscape. A well-crafted logo, website or marketing piece doesn't just look good – it stands out and attracts customers.

It also boosts your credibility. When your business looks professional and polished, people are more likely to trust you. A consistent and well-thought-out design shows you're serious about what you do, which helps in attracting a solid customer base.

Plus, good design directly influences how customers behave. A well-designed website that's easy to navigate will naturally lead to more sales because it removes barriers for users. The same goes for your marketing materials. A custom-designed flyer with clear information and a call to action will outperform a generic template every time.

Looking at the longer term, design plays a big role in building brand loyalty. Consistent branding doesn't just make your business look good – it leaves a lasting impression on customers. Over time, this helps to build trust and preference for your brand.

Design provides you with the flexibility to evolve as your market or products change. By starting with a strong design framework, you can refresh your brand as needed without incurring significant costs.

Finally, every part of your brand's design – from your logo to your website – is a business asset. As your brand becomes more recognisable, these assets grow in value, opening doors to future opportunities like partnerships or even the potential sale of your business.

Research by the Design Council shows that for every £1 spent on design, businesses can expect over £20 in increased revenue. Understanding this can change how you use your limited resources.

Investing in design builds a strong foundation for your business, driving immediate and long-term growth. While it's tempting to use DIY tools like Canva, especially for print design, professional design investment can significantly boost your revenue.

The Power of Costly Signalling

The concept of costly signalling comes from evolutionary biology and economics, where it describes actions or investments that send a credible signal about one's resources, reliability or commitment. Originally, it explained behaviours in nature, such as the peacock's elaborate tail – a costly feature that signals health and genetic quality.

In business, costly signalling refers to choices that convey commitment and quality through visible investment. In marketing, this is exemplified by using professionally designed and printed materials. High-quality brochures, business cards or signage send a message that you take your brand seriously, standing out from competitors relying on cheaper, DIY alternatives.

Well-crafted marketing materials enhance your brand's visual appeal and demonstrate your commitment to quality. For small businesses aiming to stand out, outsourcing print design to professionals is a wise choice.

In a world where first impressions matter, investing in high-quality design is a powerful way to make yours unforgettable. So, when planning your next marketing project, think beyond generic templates and drag-and-drop tools. Ask yourself, *do you want to blend in or stand out from the crowd?*

If the answer is the latter, it might be time to leave Canva behind and embrace the power of professional design.

Part 2

Stepping Up

How often do your clients ask to be featured in your marketing materials? Probably not very often. But that's exactly what happens in our family garden design business every year.

For the past few years, we've published a wall calendar that we give away to clients and suppliers. Each month showcases project photos from one of our garden transformations. The response has been overwhelmingly positive – so much so that our clients are now asking to have their gardens featured in next year's calendar. Some are even trying to reserve specific months!

So, what does this mean for our business, and how could something similar benefit yours?

From a marketing perspective, the calendar has been a game-changer. First, it strengthens our relationship with existing clients. Being featured in our calendar makes them feel valued and proud of the work we've done together. This kind of emotional connection can turn a satisfied customer into a loyal advocate who's more likely to recommend us to others.

Second, it keeps our business at the forefront of their minds all year long. Every time someone looks at the calendar, they're reminded of the our business and the quality of our work. This constant, subtle reinforcement of our brand helps us stay relevant, even when clients aren't actively looking for garden design services.

Lastly, the buzz around being featured in the calendar has created a sense of exclusivity and demand. It's no longer just a marketing tool – it's something clients aspire to be part of. This not only boosts our reputation but also encourages word-of-mouth marketing, as clients talk about their gardens and the possibility of being featured.

In simple terms, producing the calendar has helped us build stronger client relationships, maintain brand visibility and generated organic buzz around our services. It's an example of how a thoughtful, well-executed marketing tool can go beyond its initial purpose, boosting engagement and promoting long-term business growth.

This section of the book includes six print-based marketing initiatives that have the capacity to do similar things for your business. They are a little more involved than the tactics in the first section, so you might consider getting professional help – but there is also plenty here you could attempt yourself, if you want to.

10

Display Banners

Display banners are attention-grabbing, ideal for promoting events and raising brand awareness.

Let's shift gears. Up until now, we've been talking about small print items. But now it's time to think big. Really big. When you walk into a trade show or event, what's the first thing that catches your eye? It's not a business card or a flyer – it's the large, bold display graphics that dominate the space. Whether it's a pull-up banner, a poster or even a full exhibition stand, large format display graphics are all about making an impact.

For many small businesses, the focus tends to be on the smaller, everyday items – business cards, brochures and mailers. But there's a whole world of opportunity in going big. Display graphics can give your business the attention-grabbing presence it deserves, whether you're at an event, in your own retail space or showcasing your brand at a conference. This chapter is about exploring how these larger-than-life materials can attract customers, and make sure your brand doesn't just blend in – it stands out.

When I belonged to a networking organisation one of their more unusual membership benefits was that when you attended a meeting, you could put up your own roller banner at the venue.

This gave your business visibility throughout the meeting and meant that any photographs posted on social media after the event were likely to feature your branding. As the venues were often public spaces like restaurants, it meant the general public were also exposed to your advertising message.

Portable display graphics are a must-have if your business attends trade shows or expos. They also work well in shops and showrooms, offering maximum business impact at minimal cost.

Here are a few different banner systems for you to consider.

Roller Banners

Roller banners, sometimes known as pull-up banners, are probably the most popular form of portable display systems. They feature a large photographic banner that rolls into a cannister at the base. The banner is held in place with a collapsible pole, and the base usually includes small feet for stability.

They come in a range of sizes – traditional ones are two metres high and 800mm wide, but they are available up to 1500mm wide, and they can be single- or doublesided. Smaller tabletop versions in A4 and A3 sizes are available if space is at a premium – ideal for reception desks and service counters.

Roller banners are a cheap and effective option, but they are not without issues.

First, full-sized versions are awkward to put up, especially if space is limited or you are shorter than 5ft 4ins.

I've watched people try and fail to put them up in many intriguing ways. Sometimes, it's as if they were taking a windsurfing lesson. Other times, it is more like trying to watch a beginner at a pole vault competition. I've seen them get tangled up in ceiling lights and fall over when someone bumps into them.

Even I, an alleged expert, can mess it up occasionally. Once, when putting up a brand new roller banner, I accidentally let go of the graphic and it sprung back into the cannister at the base, ripping a large hole in it.

The roller's mechanism can sometimes get jammed, preventing the graphic from rolling back. Alternatively, the spring can be so tight that the graphic snaps back into the cassette with such force it invariably damages the sides of the banner.

Despite these inconveniences, the main negative issue with them is that replacing the graphics is not a simple job. This leads many people to throw away the entire cassette when their graphics go out of date – waste that goes straight to landfill.

Replacing the graphics is possible, but it is fiddly and requires patience, skill and a large, clean workspace.

Few printers currently offer recycling schemes or a replacement graphic service for roller banners, so I decided to look for alternatives. And I found one.

Canvas X-Banners

An environmentally better choice is the reusable X-frame banner stand. These consist of a lightweight tent-pole-style frame system and a separate canvas banner. The system assembles in under a minute and folds away easily for storage in a fabric case.

The printed canvas banner is held under tension by hooks in the frame. When it's time to change the graphics, you only need to replace the canvas banner, not the hardware itself, meaning less waste.

Indeed, some suppliers now offer eco-friendly compostable banner materials so you can dispose of them without a conscience. PVC banner material, however, is not recyclable or biodegradable.

X-frame banners are slightly shorter than traditional roller banners at 1800mm high but can also be up to 1200mm wide. They work well as a set, creating a continuous graphic wall when two or three are placed side by side.

Roller banners and X-frame banners are portable, so they can be left installed in your office or showroom when not required elsewhere. I've even seen people use them as backgrounds while on Zoom calls.

Neither system is suitable for external use. An outdoor X-frame stand is available, but I wouldn't recommend it – I suggest using a festival flag system instead.

Stretch Fabric Banners

An alternative option for display banners is a stretch fabric banner system. These involves printing your graphic on a polyester sleeve, which slides over a tubular frame and zips closed at the bottom.

One benefit of this system is the graphic is double-sided so you can have separate messages on each side. With its seamless graphic and dimensions up to two metres high by six metres wide, this system is perfect for conferences and trade shows, and even makes for a stunning photo wall if you wanted to hold a launch or drinks reception.

And the sleeve graphic is also washable, which is handy if your drinks reception were to get out of hand.

There are also mini table-top versions, which would be ideal for small shell-scheme stands at conferences or for reception counters.

Pop-Up Displays

This premium option is more suitable for companies who do a lot of exhibiting. Pop-up displays consist of a collapsible aluminium frame which pops up in seconds (hence the name). The frame includes in-situ magnetic fixings, which hold wrap-around graphic panels in position.

These are modular systems which allow for many different configurations. You can have double-sided systems and curved, straight or L-shaped setups. These systems give you the option to add lighting, leaflet dispensers, shelves and even attach flat-screen monitors.

The system is stored in a wheeled display case, which can itself be dressed in graphics and a wooden countertop to become a branded podium.

Pop-up prices, however, are three times those of comparable pull-ups, but the system is more robust, some coming with 10-year hardware guarantees.

Display banners are an excellent way to make your business stand out at events, trade shows and even in your own space. With the right banner, you can boost your brand visibility effectively and leave a lasting impression on your audience.

Key Takeaways

- Display graphics make a big impact at trade shows, events or in retail spaces, ensuring your brand stands out.
- Roller banners are affordable and portable but are difficult to reuse and can be wasteful.
- X-frame banners offer an eco-friendly alternative.
- Stretch fabric banners provide seamless, double-sided designs and are washable for reusability.
- Pop-up displays are premium, modular systems ideal for frequent exhibitors looking for maximum versatility.

11

Calendars

> Calendars keep your brand visible all year round, helping with awareness and customer retention. They also build reputation and keep customers engaged regularly.

Every small business owner knows the sales rhythm of the year isn't always steady. One minute, you're flat out, juggling orders and wondering how you'll keep up – the next, things slow down and you're left worrying about where your next customer will come from. These peaks and troughs are part and parcel of running a small business, no matter what industry you're in.

For my business, on the print side of things, January and August are usually dead slow. September-December are the opposite – trade shows and Christmas keep me very busy. But even if you know your own sales cycle, the frustrating reality is that customers don't buy when it's convenient for us – they buy when it's convenient for them, which is pretty selfish of them.*

And our challenge, as businesses, is that while we can predict trends, we rarely have a clear picture of exactly when a customer will be ready to buy.

---

*It's OK to think of your clients as selfish. Over 100 years ago, Claude Hopkins, American copywriter and one of the fathers of direct response marketing, had this to say about customers: *"They are selfish, as we all are. They care nothing about your interests or your profit. They seek service for themselves. Ignoring this fact is a common mistake and a costly mistake in advertising."*

So, you can appreciate the value of having a constant reminder of your business sitting on your customer's desk – something they see every day for a year. That's exactly what a simple desk calendar can do for you. It subtly keeps your business at the forefront of your customers' minds. When they find themselves in need of a product or service you offer, they're more likely to think of you first.

Why Calendars Work So Well

Calendars are more than just a functional tool for keeping track of dates. They're an understated yet powerful marketing asset. A desk calendar, for instance, becomes part of your customer's daily routine. Every time they glance at it to check a date, jot down an appointment or plan their week, they're quietly reminded of your business. This consistent visibility builds familiarity, and familiarity often leads to trust.

When your business is trusted and known, customers are more likely to reach out to you when they need something. It's not just about making a sale – it's about being the go-to option when the time is right.

The Power of Placement

Desk calendars tend to be small, and come in a range of sizes, typically A5 or DL (compliment slip size). They can be double- or single-sided and are constructed using a folded piece of card that allows them to be self-supporting. This means they take up minimal desk space but are always within easy view. By having your brand or logo visible every time your customer sits down to work, you're ensuring that your business is never far from their thoughts.

But if a desk calendar isn't quite your style, an alternative is a wall calendar. Wall calendars offer even more visibility as they often take pride of place in offices or kitchens, areas where people spend a lot of their time. Every time someone checks the date or plans their month, they'll see your brand displayed prominently.

If you have high-quality photos of your products or services, a wall calendar can showcase them beautifully, turning each month into a mini advertising campaign. You can even add QR codes to direct viewers to product pages or case studies on your website so they can find out more. That is another tactic we use in the calendar for our garden design business mentioned in the introduction to this section.

Year-Round Impact

One of the greatest strengths of a calendar as a marketing tool is its longevity. Unlike other promotional items that might be used once or twice and then forgotten, a calendar is designed to be used every day for a whole year. That's 365 days of consistent brand exposure – a level of visibility that's hard to match with other types of promotional materials.

This long life makes calendars highly cost-effective. I worked out a couple of years ago that, even if choosing the minimum order quantity, it could cost as little as 1.5p per day to have your branding sat on your clients' desks all year round. You'd be hard pressed to find advertising that cheap anywhere else.

Calendars are also practical. They help people stay organised, which means they're less likely to be discarded. When your promotional item is useful, it's more likely to be kept, and the longer it's kept, the more brand impressions, or touchpoints, it generates. Over the course of a year, those touchpoints add up, reinforcing your brand's presence in your customer's mind.

Timing Is Everything

The best time to order your calendars is in the autumn. This gives you plenty of time to plan and decide who to give them to before the Christmas rush. Calendars make excellent gifts for clients, suppliers and partners, offering a thoughtful way to say thank you while giving your business some tactful promotion.

Sending out calendars as gifts during the holiday season also aligns your brand with the spirit of giving. It's a small gesture that can make a big impact, showing your customers that you appreciate their business and value the relationship. Plus, with everyone planning for the new year, your calendar becomes a useful tool when they're setting goals and making plans.

A Calendar for Every Business

There are few promotional items that offer the utility and longevity of a calendar. Whether it's a compact desk calendar or a large wall calendar, the benefits are clear: year-round brand exposure, a useful tool for your customers, and a subtle but effective way to keep your business right under their noses.

In a world where digital marketing often takes precidence, printed calendars offer a refreshing change. They're tangible, practical, and deliver consistent value to both your business and your customers.

So, as you plan your next marketing campaign, consider the humble calendar. It might just be the long-lasting, high-impact promotional tool your business needs.

Key Takeaways

- Calendars provide daily, year-round brand visibility, keeping your business in people's minds.
- Desk calendars are compact and practical, making them a perfect addition to any workspace.
- Wall calendars showcase your branding prominently and can double as mini monthly ad campaigns.
- High-quality photos or QR codes on calendars add value and direct customers to your website.
- Their longevity makes calendars a cost-effective marketing tool, with consistent exposure over 365 days.
- Calendars are practical and appreciated, ensuring they're kept and used regularly.
- Gifting calendars in autumn or during the holiday season adds a thoughtful touch to client relationships.
- Tangible and timeless, calendars offer a refreshing change from digital marketing overload.

12

Packaging

> Packaging does more than just protect products – it boosts brand awareness and conveys important information. It can also enhance your reputation and helps position your brand in the market.

Being a superannuated constituent of Generation X, sometimes I struggle to understand millennial culture.

Case in point: I'm not sure how this happened, but young people apparently take time out of their days to watch "unboxing" videos.

The experience of unwrapping a purchase is so valuable that people film themselves doing it and upload the whole thing to YouTube.

And then other people watch it! I must be getting old.

But the more I thought about it, the more I realised that what these video bloggers are doing is showcasing just how important packaging is to the customer experience.

There is no doubt that packaging adds value. Enclosing your goods with branded stickers, wrapping paper, personalised gift tags and using boxes or bags with your own printed or stamped logo shows you have thought about your customer's experience.

In 2021, Amanda, a client of mine, launched her online confectionery brand, *Ashby Treats,* with a specific vision. When briefing me to design her logo, she said she wanted her brand to feel like it had been plucked straight from a 1950s sweet shop – a nostalgic nod to an era of glass jars, striped paper bags and simple pleasures wrapped in pastel colours. The branding brief was to evoke nostalgia, wrapping each product in the comforting familiarity of the past.

Amanda's background is as a florist, and when you step into her garden studio, you are surrounded by ribbon, wrapping paper, brown paper bags and cardboard boxes. She takes her packaging and presentation very seriously, and in one corner is a small area dedicated to taking the product photos that adorn her Etsy shop.

Thin-Slicing and the Power of Packaging

Psychologists refer to a concept called "thin-slicing" – our brain's ability to make rapid judgments based on small snippets of information. This skill allows us to form impressions quickly, often before we're even fully conscious of it. In the context of online shopping, thin-slicing is especially important. Customers make instant assessments about a product's quality, value and appeal simply from its photos. The shape, colour, and material visible in the images become subtle but persuasive cues, shaping their perception and influencing their decision to buy.

Amanda understands this well. When potential customers view her Etsy shop, they're drawn to her packages wrapped in soft pastels, brown paper and ribbon, adorned with her vintage logo. Her packaging doesn't just hold sweets – it conveys a sense of experience and care, adding value to what would otherwise be an commodity product.

The story of Amanda's packaging underscores how packaging design can shape perception. Her choice to go with a vintage aesthetic is a classic strategy in packaging psychology. Nostalgia taps into our emotions, creating an instant bond with the product by linking it to fond memories. When customers see Ashby Treats' products wrapped in retro-styled packaging, they're reminded of something familiar and trusted, even if they've never seen the brand before.

Colour and Typography: Visual Cues that Shape Perception

Beyond nostalgia, every detail on a package communicates something to the buyer. Colour is a prime example. Deep, rich colours like burgundy or emerald suggest luxury, while earthy tones and pastels can signal a natural or

homemade quality. Typography also shapes impressions – handwritten fonts, for instance, can convey personal care and craftsmanship, while bold, sans-serif type suggests modernity and professionalism.

For Ashby Treats, I chose pastel reds and greens taken from vintage sweet wrappers, combined with a script typeface meant to evoke signwriting, reinforcing the brand's charm and making it feel artisanal yet refined. Every visual element tells customers they're purchasing a small piece of the past – an indulgent experience wrapped in childhood memories.

Transparent Packaging: Building Trust

Transparency, quite literally, can build trust. When customers see the product inside, it conveys openness and quality. Clear packaging, such as glass jars or small windows in cardboard boxes, allows customers to view the product directly, which can be especially beneficial for food items like sweets.

Luxury brands have long understood that packaging can engage multiple senses to enhance perception. A textured label or embossed logo feels different in your hand and suggests quality and care. For Ashby Treats, Amanda opted for soft-touch paper for her labels and stickers, and a stamp for her logo that she can apply to brown paper bags and packing boxes.

The Personal Touch: Packaging That Feels Handcrafted

Consumers love a personal touch. A simple handwritten thank you note can make a product feel bespoke. Small, thoughtful touches like these can turn a simple product into a personalised gift, making customers feel valued and seen.

While hand-packaging every product may not be feasible, brands find clever ways to add a personal feel. From thank you notes to covering letters that use your first name, adding the human touch can make customers feel closer to your company. This works both ways – using the customer's name is highly effective, but writing from a named person within your company can have the same effect.

For example, if you buy online from the men's clothing brand Charles Tyrwhitt, you'll receive a letter soon after from their chairman thanking you for your purchase. I'm not naïve enough to think the chairman actually writes to me – but their aftersales promotion is so well considered I am quite happy to play along with this pretence, especially as it comes with a money-off code for future purchases.

Sustainability: An Ethical and Strategic Choice

Today's consumers are increasingly conscious of environmental impact, and packaging is a key concern. Amanda took this to heart with Ashby Treats, using kraft paper and recyclable materials. Each shipment includes a small card detailing Amanda's "packaging promise," explaining her sustainable material choices and encouraging customers to reuse or recycle the packaging.

Incorporating sustainable materials not only resonates with customers who value greener choices but also helps build brand trust. Small businesses like Ashby Treats can make a significant impact by choosing options such as recycled cardboard, compostable bags or reusable glass jars, all of which enhance a positive brand image.

This can work the other way for brands, too – I stopped ordering from HelloFresh a few years ago because the amount of packaging waste was unacceptable, and I stopped buying Dolce Gusto coffee pods for the same reason.

Beyond aesthetics, practical packaging choices make a difference in the supply chain. Small businesses benefit from materials that are stackable, lightweight and cost-effective to post. Amanda's choice of kraft paper bags and simple, stackable boxes means she can keep shipping costs low while maintaining her brand's vintage appeal. By choosing efficient and visually appealing designs, businesses can optimise for both branding and practicality.

Eco-Friendly Packaging Materials

Several materials fit the bill for sustainable packaging.

Bioplastics, for instance, are made from plant-based materials like sugar cane or corn, and they're biodegradable, making them an excellent choice for items like bags, wrapping and containers.

Cardboard is another reliable option – it's durable, reusable and widely recycled. To ensure your cardboard is responsibly sourced, look for FSC or PEFC certification.

Paper packaging is similar to cardboard in its environmental friendliness – it's renewable, biodegradable and highly recyclable. Again, opting for FSC-certified paper guarantees that the materials come from well-managed forests or recycled sources.

Fabric bags made from materials like jute, cotton or hemp offer a reusable and eco-friendly alternative, and they can be responsibly disposed of at the end of their life.

If you're looking for something more innovative, **mushroom packaging** could be the answer. This natural material, made from mycelium, is biodegradable and serves as a fantastic replacement for expanded polystyrene. It's suitable for packaging bottles, plants, and even gift boxes.

Glass is another excellent choice – it can be infinitely recycled without losing quality and is perfect for preserving product integrity while allowing customers to see what's inside.

Lastly, **bamboo** is gaining popularity due to its low cost, sustainability and compostability, making it an ideal material for packaging in industries like cosmetics, clothing and food.

The Silent Power of Packaging

Packaging is more than just a container – it's a silent salesperson. Amanda's story proves that thoughtfully designed packaging can transform an ordinary product into an experience, building anticipation and forming a lasting impression before the first sweet is even tasted. When customers receive a package from Ashby Treats, they aren't just buying sweets – they're buying a memory, an emotion, a slice of the past wrapped in a modern business's commitment to quality and sustainability.

Key Takeaways

- Thoughtful packaging enhances the customer experience and creates a lasting impression of your brand.
- Packaging design influences perception through colour, typography and materials that reflect your brand's values.
- Transparent packaging builds trust by showcasing the product directly and conveying openness.
- Adding personal touches like handwritten notes or stamped logos can make customers feel valued.
- Sustainable packaging materials like kraft paper, recycled cardboard or glass appeal to eco-conscious consumers and boost brand trust.
- Practical choices like stackable, lightweight materials optimise shipping costs while maintaining aesthetic appeal.
- High-quality, well-designed packaging reinforces your brand's identity and signal your commitment to quality.

13

Greetings Cards

> Greetings cards can lend your marketing the personal touch, strengthening customer retention and brand awareness.

Spare a thought for the poor souls whose birthdays fall on February 14th.

That's exactly the fate of one of my old bosses.

"Being born on Valentine's Day," she would complain every year, "is a nightmare. You can't get a table in a restaurant without having to pay double and book weeks in advance."

But, beyond being a day that causes headaches for those born on it, Valentine's Day is a dream for marketers. It sits perfectly between the post-Christmas lull and the lead-up to Easter, providing businesses with a timely opportunity to boost sales during a quiet period. Retailers, florists, restaurants and chocolatiers all cash in, but even companies far removed from love and romance find ways to use it. Take Siteground, the web hosting provider, who once boldly advertised a 75% discount on their hosting services as the ultimate Valentine's gift.

Who says romance is dead?

Valentine's Day, however, isn't the only time we exchange cards. As businesses, we should be taking full advantage of any opportunity to send cards to our customers, whether for birthdays, holidays or other special occasions. It's an often-overlooked marketing tool that can make a lasting impression.

Religious Holidays

Whether you're religious or not, some of your customers may be, so sending cards for certain religious holidays can be a thoughtful touch. The most popular in the UK, of course, is Christmas – businesses have been sending branded Christmas cards to customers for decades. It's a small gesture that can have a big impact, helping you stay connected and show a little appreciation.

Most businesses stick to Christmas and Easter, but why stop there? The UK is a diverse nation, and recognising other religious holidays like Eid and Diwali can help you stand out. Eid al-Fitr marks the end of Ramadan, and Diwali, the festival of lights, is a perfect opportunity to reach out with a thoughtful message. It shows you're paying attention and that you're respectful of your customers' different backgrounds.

You don't need to get too religious with your messaging, either. Instead of sticking to specific greetings, you can go for something more inclusive like "Wishing you joy and prosperity" or "Warm wishes for the season" during the winter holidays. That way, your cards can work for all your customers, no matter what their beliefs are.

And don't forget about other holidays that might resonate with your audience – Rosh Hashanah, the Jewish New Year in autumn, or Vaisakhi, the Sikh New Year in April, could be great opportunities to reach out too. A well-timed card is a simple, low-cost way to show you care and keep your business on your customers' radar.

Awareness Days

For businesses that think they don't have a product or service that aligns with traditional or religious holidays, the calendar is full of other opportunities. Awareness days, for example, offer a chance to connect with your audience in a meaningful way.

These days range from serious United Nations sanctioned campaigns like *World Autism Awareness Day* on April 2nd, to quirky ones like *World Naked Gardening Day* on May 7th, which, while ridiculous (and far too cold), can be a fun way to grab attention.

The beauty of these days is that they give you a reason to get in touch and remind your customers that you're thinking of them. If you can't find a suitable awareness day, you can create your own. Take *International Talk Like a Pirate Day* on September 19th. It started as a joke between friends, but it went viral and even caught the attention of big organisations. Marie Curie Cancer Care, for instance, used it to run a successful fundraising campaign.

The lesson here is that with a bit of creativity, you can invent a reason to connect with your customers, it doesn't have to be tied to an established holiday, and it can be as serious or frivolous as you like.

Thank You

If all else fails, and you can't find or create a special day that aligns with your business, there's always the simple yet powerful thank you card.

A study from the University of Texas discovered that customers who receive a thank you card are 42% more likely to buy again. Meanwhile, a survey by SmallBizTrends showed that 68% of customers stop using a business because they feel the company doesn't care about them.

Sending thank you cards is a simple way to counter this and build stronger relationships with your clients.

For charities, sending handwritten thank you cards has been proven to improve donor retention.

A thank you note expressing gratitude is a rarity these days, making it all the more special when it arrives in your customer's post. This small gesture can set you apart from your competition, showing your clients that you value them as more than just a transaction.

Bespoke or Purchased Cards?

When it comes to sending cards, you've got two main options: you can go all out and have custom cards designed to match your brand's personality, or you can opt for pre-printed cards that still carry a heartfelt message. Either way, your customers will appreciate the effort.

Sending a card is also the perfect chance to sneak in a referral incentive. Imagine your customer's surprise when they open the card to find a note that says, "Thanks for your recent order! If you recommend a friend, we'll give you both 20% off your next purchase." It's a small touch that not only makes your customer feel valued but also encourages them to bring new business your way. A win-win!

It's a well-known fact that it's easier (and cheaper) to market to existing customers than to constantly chase new ones. A thank you card does more than just say thanks – it's a way to keep the relationship alive. It's a friendly reminder to your customers of why they chose you in the first place and why they should keep coming back.

In a world full of emails and texts, a physical card really stands out. It's something your customer can hold, maybe even display, and it feels much more personal. When was the last time you got a handwritten card from a business? If you start sending them, you'll quickly become one of the few who do. It's a simple way to show your customers that they matter – and that kind of gesture goes a long way.

Key Takeaways

- Greeting cards provide a personal touch that helps your business stand out in a digital world.
- Sending cards for holidays, birthdays or awareness days shows thoughtfulness and keeps your brand visible.
- Inclusive messaging on cards ensures they resonate with diverse audiences without alienating anyone.
- Awareness days or quirky celebrations offer creative opportunities to connect with customers meaningfully.
- Thank you cards help create loyalty, showing customers they're valued beyond their transactions.
- Custom-designed cards reflect your brand's personality, while pre-printed ones still carry impact.

14

Point of Sale

POS and POP materials directly influence sales by encouraging purchases and cross-selling. They also help educate customers about products and engage them right at the decision point.

I have tried to keep industry jargon to a minimum throughout this book, but sometimes it is unavoidable. So, bear with me while I introduce the rather confusingly named **POS** and **POP**.

If you have retail premises, this is the chapter for you!

POS (Point of Sale) is advertising and promotional materials placed specifically at the checkout area, where sales transactions occur. POS is typically small in size.

POP (Point of Purchase) refers to the marketing materials and displays found throughout the rest of the store, often near the products on shelves or in display areas. These are designed to influence purchasing decisions as customers browse and tend to be larger.

Let's explore each in turn.

Point of Sale

The purpose of POS is to highlight offers and advertise specific products. It's used to upsell customers and increase their spending per visit.

It's not the place for airy-fairy brand awareness or reams of features and benefits. Because of its location, POS is usually small, so messaging needs to be on point.

Here are a few ideas for POS materials – if you have retail space, see which ones could work for you.

Counter Displays

These are small displays placed on the checkout counter, often featuring smaller, impulse-buy items like chewing gum, mints or batteries. They're designed to catch the customer's eye while they wait to pay. If you produce small gift items, think about creating counter display packaging for them, and encourage your stockists to display them at the till.

Receipt Holders

Branded holders or sleeves for receipts often include coupons, promotions for future purchases or product information, keeping your brand in the customer's mind even after they leave the store. If your receipts are sheets of A4, printed on an inkjet under the counter, you're missing a trick if you don't put them in a branded receipt holder.

Loyalty Programme Signage

These signs promote your store's loyalty scheme, encouraging customers to sign up or use their points during the checkout process, thus driving repeat business.

Menu Holders

Also known as talkers, these simple free-standing frames allow you to display important information on sales counters and tables, such as menus or discounts. Chalkboard versions of these can enable you to create and update your offers very quickly.

Dump Bins

Free-standing polypropylene or cardboard dump-bins, either floor-standing or for countertops, are another great way to encourage impulse buys. They can be easily branded with your sales message.

Promotional Stickers

Small stickers or decals applied directly to the counter surface can promote a special offer, remind customers of a limited-time deal or reinforce a brand message right at the point of sale.

Point of Purchase

Moving away from the sales counter, we enter the world of Point of Purchase, or POP.

POP promotional printing serves as a crucial tool for SMEs aiming to grab customer attention right where purchasing decisions are made.

This marketing strategy involves creating vivid, eye-catching printed materials placed around the products. It effectively highlights offers, guides consumer choices, and can significantly boost sales figures without the high costs associated with large-scale advertising campaigns.

Wobblers

These are small graphics fixed to shelving systems with a flexible piece of acrylic, so they wobble when touched. The movement makes them eye-catching, and they don't get in the way of the merchandise. They are ideal for promoting discounts, BOGOF (buy one get one free) offers and prompting impulse purchases.

Posters

Suspended poster hangers and hanging snap frames allow you to position posters above your merchandise and are also used for window displays. They are perfect for sale posters and easy to keep updated.

Standees

A standee is a freestanding display, printed onto lightweight corrugated cardboard or sometimes plastic, which stands on the shop floor alongside a new product or promotion. It's possible to cut them into elaborate shapes, and because of their unusual appearance, they attract attention.

In my former life as an agency graphic designer, I designed standees for supermarket displays, motorcycle showrooms and exhibitions.

As you've hopefully realised by now, this book is all about standing out and attracting attention for your business. If you've ever seen a life-size cardboard cut-out of a police officer near a supermarket entrance, you get the idea how effective they are at catching your eye.

Sometimes standees can include a sample of the new product. A few years ago, I was involved in creating some standees for Bridgestone when they launched a new motorcycle tyre in the UK.

As well as displaying the new tyre's features and benefits, at its centre was an actual full-size tyre.

Smaller POS standees can be produced for countertops or service desks.

Standees might only be relevant to you if you have a retail sales space. But if you do, and your standees are striking enough, they are a great way of flagging up a new product and starting a sales conversation.

Look Down

Floor graphics are yet another innovative POP solution, ideal for directing customers to specific products or areas within a store. These are particularly useful during specific promotions or seasonal sales.

As I mentioned in the Stickers chapter, I once was involved in designing floor graphics for the Škoda Yeti car launch, and these involved huge sticker in the shape of footprints leading from the entrance to the new models in the showroom. Because stickers can be any shape, they can be used for eye-catching graphics, such as splashes and flames.

For SMEs in retail, or for those producing retail products, these POP materials not only stimulate sales but also enhance brand recognition. By placing engaging and informative displays at critical decision points, you can effectively guide the purchasing process, making POP an invaluable tool for boosting visibility and sales in-store.

Key Takeaways

- Point of Sale materials like counter displays and dump bins drive impulse purchases and promote offers right at the checkout.
- Point of Purchase materials, such as posters and wobblers, highlight products and offers on the shop floor where buying decisions are made.
- Freestanding displays like standees grab attention, especially for new products or seasonal promotions.
- Floor graphics can guide customers to specific products or areas, creating a dynamic and interactive shopping experience.

15

Flyers

> Flyers are versatile and can effectively raise brand awareness, drive sales and promote events. They're also useful for direct responses, generating leads and introducing new products or services.

I couldn't write a book on print-based marketing and not talk about flyers.

Flyers (or leaflets if you prefer) are one of the most versatile tools in marketing, and I honestly believe every business can find a use for them. Whether you're looking to get the word out about your company, promote a new product or raise awareness for a service, flyers are a tried-and-tested way to go about it.

Yet, despite their potential, many businesses shy away from using them.

Some argue that printing them is wasteful: "I printed thousands, and I've still got boxes left over." or "They go out of date too quickly." But these issues are not a fault of the flyers themselves – they are more about how the flyers are distributed and managed.

So, let's think about flyers in a different way.

Incoming Analogy Alert! Stand By!

Consider the humble dandelion.

Each dandelion flower produces around 180 seeds, and each plant can have up to eight flower heads. Throughout the year, as these plants continue blooming, they eventually produce up to 5,000 seeds in a single season. Now, how do these seeds spread? They rely on the wind to carry them far and wide, sometimes as much as five miles from the parent plant.

Most of these seeds will not survive. Many will land on hard ground, others will be eaten and some will simply dry out. But a few lucky ones will land on fertile soil, take root and grow into new plants. Mission accomplished!

If you've ever tended a lawn, you'll know how effective a dandelions' seed distribution system is.

Flyers work in much the same way. To be effective, they need to be widely distributed and done so regularly. Once your flyers are out there, you don't have control over exactly where they'll end up or who will grab one. But, just like those dandelion seeds, some of your flyers will reach the right place – in the hands of those who are interested in what your business has to offer.

This is why you shouldn't hesitate to distribute flyers in large quantities. It's a numbers game, much like it is for the dandelion. The more flyers you distribute, the better your chances of reaching potential customers. And remember, you're not just aiming for a single response from each flyer. A well-placed flyer can generate multiple leads if it finds its way to a notice-board, each lead potentially becoming a sale.

The Cost Factor

Another great reason to lean towards volume when it comes to flyers is cost efficiency.

Without diving too deep into the principles of fixed versus variable costs, here's a simplified version: When you print a small number of flyers (or anything else), a significant portion of the cost is spent just getting the job on the printing press. This setup cost is fixed, meaning it's the same whether you print 50 flyers or 50,000. Once the press is running, the cost of producing each additional flyer is mostly just the cost of the paper and ink, which is relatively cheap.

For example, if a printer offers you 200 flyers for £20, that's 10p per flyer. But if you increase your order to 2,000 flyers, the total cost might only go up to £50. Now you're down to a unit price of 2.5p. And if you decide to really go big and order 20,000 flyers, you might pay £260, bringing the cost per flyer down to just 1.3p.

This sliding scale of affordability is what makes flyers perfect for mass distribution. The more you print, the cheaper each flyer becomes. And since flyers are all about numbers, being able to print large quantities at a low cost gives you the best chance of success.

Staying Power

According to the Data and Marketing Association, 45% of people save flyers for future reference, which says a lot about the longevity of print marketing. Flyers aren't just fleeting – they have a staying power that keeps your message in front of potential customers long after a digital ad would have disappeared. Whether pinned to a noticeboard or saved in a drawer, they serve as a physical reminder of your business and what you offer.

Mass Distribution: The Dandelion Strategy

Nature has it figured out. If dandelions only produced a handful of seeds with the hope that every one would turn into a new plant, they'd be extinct by now. Instead, they produce thousands of seeds to ensure that enough of them will find their way to fertile ground.

Your business should take a similar approach. By opting for mass distribution, you're increasing your chances of reaching more people, which in turn increases your chances of spreading awareness and gaining new customers.

Flyers also offer flexibility in how you target your audience. You can distribute them in specific locations where your target market is likely to be, such as local events, busy shopping areas or through direct mail. You can have them delivered with other flyers, or with local magazines. Alternatively, you can select addresses and use a targeted delivery service. They can be used to promote time-sensitive offers, special events or simply to raise awareness of your brand.

When you combine the low cost of printing with the wide reach that flyers offer, it's easy to see why they remain a popular choice for businesses of all sizes. They give you the ability to connect with your audience in a tangible way, something digital marketing can't replicate.

So, take a page out of nature's book. Just like the dandelion ensures its survival through mass distribution, ensure your business thrives by getting your message out there through a well-executed flyer campaign.

Key Takeaways

- Flyers are a versatile and cost-effective tool for promoting products, services or events.
- Distributing flyers widely increases your chances of reaching potential customers, much like dandelion seeds finding fertile soil.
- Printing in larger quantities reduces the cost per flyer, improving cost efficiency and making it easier to reach more customers affordably.
- Flyers offer flexibility in targeting, whether through local events, direct mail or specific delivery services.
- They can be used for time-sensitive promotions, awareness campaigns or simply to boost visibility.
- A well-placed flyer can generate multiple leads, especially if displayed on noticeboards or shared among customers.
- Unlike digital marketing, flyers provide a tangible and long-lasting connection with your audience.
- Consistent and regular distribution is key to maximising the impact of a flyer campaign.

Intermission

The Power of Touchpoints

Running a business isn't just about offering great products or services. It's about the entire experience your customers have with your brand, and that experience is shaped by every interaction, big or small. These interactions, known as touchpoints, are the building blocks of your brand's image in the minds of your customers.

For small businesses, effectively managing these touchpoints - and increasing their number - can make the difference between attracting (or not attracting) a prospect and gaining a customer who becomes a loyal advocate for your company.

Building customer relationships is a lot like forming a close friendship - you can't expect a lifelong bond from just one meeting. It takes time, trust and multiple meaningful interactions to reach that level of connection.

First Impressions and Follow-Ups

The first customer touchpoint is a bit like a first date. It could be the moment a potential customer lands on your website, sees an ad or walks into your shop. Just like in dating, first impressions matter. You wouldn't show up late or give one-word answers on a first date (I hope).

In the same way, you want that first interaction with your business to be welcoming, engaging and memorable. It's your chance to show what your business is all about and make your prospect feel like they've found something special.

But one good interaction isn't enough to seal the deal. After that first date, it's crucial to keep the momentum going. Maybe it's a follow-up email, a thoughtful blog post or a personalised recommendation. This stage is like the early dating period when you're getting to know someone. You don't want to be too pushy, but you also don't want them to forget about you. Thoughtful, consistent communication shows your potential customers that you're serious about earning their trust and their business.

Commitment and Beyond

Once you've built up enough trust, the customer eventially makes the decision to buy from you. It's like taking that next big step in a relationship – moving in together or becoming an item. But just as in dating, this decision isn't the end of the story. The real work begins now.

In any good relationship, the effort you put in after the commitment is what makes things last. The same goes for customer relationships. After a purchase, follow-up touchpoints – like asking how they're getting on with their purchase, offering tips or sending a thank you note – are essential. These small gestures reinforce the relationship, showing that you care about more than just the sale.

The ultimate goal is to turn a one-time buyer into a long-term customer who not only sticks around but also becomes an advocate for your brand. These are the customers who tell others about how great you are, leaving positive reviews or referring their friends and family. Every interaction after the sale, from a helpful customer service chat to an exclusive offer, strengthens this bond.

The Power of Multiple Touchpoints

Studies show that it often takes multiple interactions before a customer decides to buy. Depending on your product or service, it could take anywhere from seven to twenty touchpoints before a prospect becomes a paying customer. I read recently that it can take over 150 exposures to a book cover on Amazon before a potential buyer clicks on it.

Take buying a car, for example. Few people walk into a dealership and buy the first model they see. Instead, they do research, read reviews, browse websites, maybe even request brochures or ask for advice from friends.

In our garden design business, we've had clients who've read every single page of our website – even going back through 15 years of blog posts – before getting in touch. By the time they do, they've gone a long way to convincing themselves they are ready to buy because of all those small interactions that earned their trust along the way.

And these touchpoints aren't just important before the sale. Every interaction, whether it happens before, during or after a purchase, contributes to the overall customer journey. That's why consistency across all your touchpoints – whether it's your website, your social media or in printed marketing – is so crucial. Consistent messaging, tone and quality help build trust and make your brand more recognisable, which is key to standing out among the competition.

Turning Touchpoints into Action

Every touchpoint in your customer journey should have a purpose – and that purpose is often to move the customer closer to taking action. Whether it's clicking a button, filling out a form or making a purchase, a clear and compelling call to action (CTA) ensures that customers know what to do next. For SMEs, this means mapping out each stage of the journey and providing CTAs that are both relevant to the customer's needs and aligned with your goals. For example, a website homepage might prompt visitors to "Explore Our Services," while a follow-up email could encourage them to "Book a Discovery Call."

The key to an effective CTA is making it super-easy and enticing for the customer to act. Use action-oriented language and ensure the steps are straightforward – no one wants to wade through a complicated process or an enormous form to get what they need. CTAs don't have to be limited to digital interactions, either. A flyer can invite recipients to "Visit Us Today," while a thank you card might suggest they "Leave a Review." By including a clear next step at every touchpoint, you not only keep customers engaged but also guide them seamlessly through their journey, from first contact to long-term loyalty.

Key Customer Touchpoints to Consider

Small business owners often don't think of marketing as an ongoing process, treating it more like a series of one-off activities. But marketing is something that should be happening continuously, as it affects every stage of the customer journey.

Here are some important touchpoints that can either strengthen your relationship with a customer – or, if done poorly, weaken it.

- **Your Company Website**: Often the first point of contact, customers come here to learn about your offerings, your values and why they should choose you.
- **Social Media Profiles**: Social media allows for more personal interaction. This is often where customers first engage with your brand and stay updated.
- **Email Marketing**: A direct line to your audience, email lets you nurture leads, share valuable content, and inform customers about promotions. Importantly, this is a channel you own and control.
- **Local Events and Sponsorships**: Participating in local events helps build personal connections and increase brand awareness in your community.
- **Google Business Listing**: A well-maintained profile boosts your local search visibility and provides essential information.
- **Customer Reviews and Testimonials**: These act as social proof, reassuring potential customers that others have had positive experiences.
- **Printed Marketing Materials**: All the print items in this book are tangible touchpoints that make your brand memorable and help reinforce your message.
- **Customer Service Interactions**: Every time a customer interacts with your service team, it's a chance to build or lose trust.
- **Loyalty Programmes**: Designed to keep customers engaged and coming back, loyalty programmes create additional touchpoints through rewards, exclusive offers and personalised customer experiences.
- **Referrals and Word of Mouth**: The most powerful touchpoints come from satisfied customers recommending your business to others.

Touchpoints for Lapsed Customers

Building relationships with customers isn't just about acquiring new ones, but also about reconnecting with those who haven't interacted with your business in a while. Lapsed customers represent a valuable opportunity, as they're already familiar with your brand, making it easier and more cost-effective to re-engage them than to attract brand-new prospects. A thoughtful touchpoint strategy can help rekindle their interest and encourage these customers to return, reminding them of the value your business provides.

One effective way to re-engage lapsed customers is through personalised communication. Sending an email or printed piece that acknowledges the gap – such as "We've missed you!" – along with a special offer or incentive, can make them feel valued. A discount code, an exclusive promotion or an invitation to a loyalty programme might be enough to re-establish the connection. Additionally, providing a reason for them to engage, like sharing updates on new products, services or success stories, can spark their interest in your business again.

Don't underestimate the power of non-promotional touchpoints as well. A simple thank you note, seasonal greetings or even a survey asking for feedback can be effective. These gestures show that you care about the relationship beyond just sales and remind them why they chose your business. By combining personalised offers with genuine, thoughtful interactions, you create a compelling reason for lapsed customers to reconnect.

Overcoming Common Touchpoint Challenges

Small businesses often struggle with managing touchpoints effectively, usually because of limited resources or inconsistent messaging. One common issue is an over-reliance on just a few marketing channels, like social media, while neglecting others, such as print, email marketing or customer service. To succeed, you need to diversify your efforts and make sure every touchpoint is working together.

Another issue is inconsistent branding. Without following clear guidelines for things like logos, colours and messaging, your touchpoints can feel disconnected, which can confuse customers and dilute your brand.

And of course, many small businesses don't take the time to fully map out their customer journey, leading to missed opportunities to engage customers at crucial moments.

To overcome these challenges, create a marketing plan that anticipates customer needs at each stage of the journey, ensures consistent branding across all touchpoints, and measures what's working and what's not.

Print Marketing: Tangible Touchpoints

While digital marketing tends to dominate SME thinking, print marketing plays a vital role in any well-rounded strategy. It's a handwritten note in an age of text messages – it's personal, tangible and stands out. A well-designed business card or brochure adds a physical layer to your touchpoints, something customers can hold onto long after they've left your website or stopped scrolling.

For small businesses, print marketing can serve as the bridge between online engagement and real-world interaction. When a customer receives a thoughtfully crafted thank you card after a purchase or is handed an eye-catching brochure at a local event, these touchpoints create memorable experiences that digital marketing alone can't replicate.

When print marketing is seamlessly integrated into your broader strategy, it reinforces your brand's consistency and leaves a lasting impression. It's not just an add-on – it's a powerful tool for building relationships and driving long-term loyalty.

Touchpoints, Trust and Lasting Relationships

Like any good relationship, building trust with your customers takes time and effort. The journey doesn't end with the sale, just as a relationship doesn't end after your wedding day. By nurturing your touchpoints – both online and offline – you're not only creating a strong first impression but also laying the groundwork for long-term loyalty.

Remember, every interaction is a chance to build or break trust. Whether it's through a well-timed email, a helpful social media post or a carefully designed piece of print marketing, your touchpoints are the key to turning a casual interaction into a meaningful, lasting relationship.

Part 3

The Big League

Many of the print marketing activities in this book have a short to medium-term shelf life. But some of the tactics in this final section can last for years.

One of them is branding your work vehicle. In our family garden design business, our first van had the ghost of the previous owner's vinyl graphic faded into the paintwork. If you'd looked closely, you might have questioned why garden design services were being provided by Interserve.

When we replaced that van, we spent £500 on signwriting, which was a big investment for us at that time. But over the next five years, we could directly attribute £20,000 of business to customers who contacted us having seen the van – a return on investment of 3,900%.

We'd leave the vehicle in highly visible areas. If we used a public car park, we'd choose the end of a row to maximise exposure, and it worked.

Van graphics, and the other activities in this section, are highly specialised and should not be considered DIY projects. The single exception to that is writing books, which is covered in the final chapter.

These tactics are either more costly, or time-consuming, or both, which is why they are in a separate section. They will require investment and professional help. But they can all serve your business well.

Protein Wisdom by Sean Hickin – used under a CC-BY 2.0 Attribution licence https://www.flickr.com/photos/sean_hickin/3053917962/in/album-72157632153323199/

16

Vehicle Graphics

> Vehicle graphics turn your cars and vans into moving adverts, boosting brand awareness and market reach. They also help position your brand within specific geographic areas.

We're in the "expensive" section now, so to begin, we're going to take a brief excursion to examine the history of mobile marketing – the human billboard.

Carrying signs and wearing advertising hoardings has a long and colourful history, and one noteworthy, but barely known, practitioner was Stanley Green.

In the late 1960s, Stanley began his mobile advertising career in my hometown of Harrow, in the sleepy suburbs of northwest London.

A practical chap, it didn't take him long to realise there were better venues for campaigning than outside Sopers department store. So, he got on his bike and pedalled the 12 miles to London's premier tourist trap, Oxford Street, where he became part of the furniture for the next twenty-five years.

Stanley's mission was to patrol the pavement six days a week with a large sign warning us all to "LUST LESS BY LESS PROTEIN." If you couldn't dodge him, he'd try to sell you a home-printed pamphlet titled *Eight Passion Proteins With Care*. In it, he argued that avoiding meat, fish, eggs, nuts and similar foods (and also sitting) was essential to save Britain from carnal collapse into Moral Turpitude.

While this may seem an unusual and rather pathetic way to spread his message, by 1993 he'd sold 87,000 pamphlets. Whether London's West End was less lustful as a result remains unclear.

As a human billboard, Stanley Green was not alone. He rubbed shoulders with dozens of other 'sandwich men', as Charles Dickens described them a century before. They infested Piccadilly Circus, Leicester Square and Tottenham Court Road with kindly invitations to HOT CHINESE BUFFETS, HALF-PRICE TANNING, CLOSING DOWN GOLF SALES, COMPUTER FAIRS, TOP QUALITY SOFAS (Direct from the Factory) and POSH LEATHER & SHEEPSKIN DESIGNER WEAR.

London's lowly sandwich men (and latterly, women) had been a fixture in the city for nearly 200 years until 2008, when Westminster Council banned them. A councillor, Daniel Astaire, commented, apparently without a hint of irony, "This is a world-class city, not a junkyard."

I don't know your opinions about proteins, and I'm certainly not suggesting you strap advertising boards to yourself and march up and down your local high street (although if you fancy it, don't let me stop you). But the idea of mobile advertising and getting your brand out among the people has (I'm so sorry) got legs.

The most effective way for you to do this (which Westminster Council has yet to ban) is to add branded advertising to your car or van.

There are three options to do this. The cheapest way is to use magnetic panels. The more traditional method is to go for cut vinyl lettering, while the most expensive route is to invest in a full vehicle wrap.

Whichever you choose, vehicle graphics are among the most cost-effective and visible ways of publicising your business.

Low-Budget: Magnetic Panels

Magnetic panels are a cheap and flexible way to add branding to your car or van. They're thin, durable and easy to remove and re-apply, making them a great option if you lease your vehicle, as they don't damage your paintwork.

You can create them in custom shapes, so they don't have to be boring, bland rectangles. You can even try to complement the colour of your car's bodywork.

When using magnetic panels on your vehicle, you are restricted by the size of individual bodywork panels and, as they are magnetic, they don't stick to plastic bodywork or glass. This limitation means you often don't have a lot of space to include things like long web addresses, but this is where a QR code comes in handy.

I have a client who is an online optician. He uses a QR code on his branded magnetic panels, so shoppers can scan the code to visit his online shop wherever his car is parked, which is frequently outside his local branch of Specsavers! I do love a bit of guerrilla marketing.

Medium Budget: Cut Vinyl Lettering

If you don't wish to be constrained by the panel sizes of your car's bodywork, you can use cut vinyl lettering to sign-write your vehicle instead. Otherwise known as decals, cut vinyl lettering allows you a bit more creative freedom. You can extend your messaging over the entire length of your car and apply them to windows too if you wish.

Cut vinyl graphics are made from a thin, self-adhesive film that is die-cut and supplied on a backing sheet – rather like grown-up versions of the stickers we had as kids. The graphics are applied to your vehicle's paintwork by carefully using a squeegee to ensure there are no trapped air bubbles.

I don't recommend you do this yourself, but if you do, you'll need patience, a steady hand and clean bodywork before you begin. They are a nightmare to reposition if you get it wrong, so I suggest getting a specialist body shop to do it for you.

Vinyl is durable and long-lasting and will survive the elements as well as repeated trips through the car wash. However, when removed, they can leave a trace on your paintwork if not done carefully.

Big-Budget: Vehicle Wraps

If you want your car or van (or bus, lorry or cement mixer) to make a big impact, you need a vehicle wrap. Whatever your mode of transport, wrapping can cover it entirely or just a part of it. Vehicle wraps involve printing your advertising graphics on large vinyl sheets, which are applied to the bodywork and then heat-treated in position.

Applying wraps is definitely not a DIY job. It should be undertaken by a specialist body shop, who may also create the graphics for you, as they will need to be designed to accommodate the curved surfaces of your bodywork.

Wrapping Glass for Privacy

Vehicle glass can be wrapped using **Contra Vision**, a special vinyl with micro-holes that allows light in and lets you see out. Applied to the outside of the glass, it displays your branding as a one-way graphic while keeping the interior private. It's a smart way to extend your message without losing functionality (just don't use it on your windscreen).

The Benefits of Vehicle Graphics

Vehicle graphics give your brand visibility wherever you go, often attracting attention even when you're off duty. Arriving at appointments or job sites in a branded vehicle adds credibility, showing you're serious and invested in your business – setting you apart from anonymous white van drivers. Including logos for trade accreditations can further boost trust and professionalism.

For local businesses, vehicle graphics raise your profile in the community, and they're incredibly cost-effective. Unlike ongoing digital or print ad costs, a one-time investment in vehicle graphics keeps promoting your business for years.

So, whatever your business, even if you're flogging posh sheepskin coats or campaigning for the suppression of desire among degenerate Londoners, mobile advertising works, and your vehicle is the perfect place for it.

Key Takeaways

- Vehicle graphics turn your car or van into a mobile advertisement, a durable, long-lasting investment providing constant visibility wherever you go.
- Branded vehicles convey professionalism and credibility, making your business stand out from unmarked competitors.
- They are especially effective for local businesses, raising your profile within the community.

17

Catalogues

Catalogues showcase your offerings, drive sales and encourage cross-selling. They're also effective for raising brand awareness, engaging customers and generating leads.

What's the difference between a brochure and a catalogue?

On the surface, the distinction might seem minor – perhaps it's simply that companies offering services lean towards brochures, while those selling products opt for catalogues.

But whatever definitions we choose, we all have a pretty clear idea of what a catalogue should look like. It needs to be comprehensive, well-produced, filled with enticing photos and detailed information that showcases your products. It should also be easy to navigate, guiding customers seamlessly from browsing to buying with clear instructions on how to place an order.

Now, I'm going to stick my neck out: a catalogue is one of those printed marketing materials that you should NEVER consider creating yourself.

Yes, you heard that right. I know the temptation is there – after all, with so many DIY design tools available, it's easy to think you can save a few quid by taking the reins yourself. But it's a bad idea.

"Yes, but Keith," I hear you cry, "you would say that, wouldn't you?"

You're right – I would. But not because I'm just trying to drum up business. I'm speaking from experience, having designed countless catalogues over the years, and I can tell you with absolute certainty – getting a catalogue right is no walk in the park. It's a long and complex, detail-oriented task that demands a professional touch, and here's why that matters.

Think back to the 1970s and 80s, when catalogues were a big thing. My mum would spend hours thumbing through the Littlewoods home shopping catalogue, which was practically a household staple. And who could forget the Argos catalogue, especially at Christmas? It was like a book of mythical treasures, eagerly anticipated and pored over by children and adults alike.

Fast forward a few years, and the Next Directory was so polished it could easily double as a coffee table book. Even today, catalogues like Screwfix's offer a fascinating glimpse into the world of DIY, sparking the imagination of hobbyists and professionals alike.

What all these examples have in common is that they were more than just booklets filled with products. They were meticulously crafted marketing tools, designed not just to inform, but to inspire and persuade. They had high production values – the design, layout, photography and content all working together to create a compelling narrative that draws the reader in and makes them want to buy.

Achieving that level of quality takes more than just a good eye for layout – it takes experience, expertise and a deep understanding of how to connect with your audience.

Catalogues are important not just because they're comprehensive, but because they represent a significant investment in time and money. If you cut corners by attempting a DIY approach, you risk ending up with a catalogue that looks amateurish, confuses your customers, and ultimately fails to deliver sales.

A poorly designed catalogue can do more harm than good, undermining your brand's credibility and costing you customers in the long run.

So, when it comes to creating a catalogue for your business, leave it to the professionals. It's an investment that will pay off handsomely, ensuring that your catalogue is not just a functional tool, but a powerful asset that showcases your products in the best possible light and drives your business forward.

My Life As A Catalogue Designer

In the design world, as in life, if you do something well, you keep being asked to do it again. You do not want to become pigeonholed as the Go-To Designer for something you hate doing. Throughout my 25-year industry career, I

A few of the many catalogues I've had a hand in producing.

managed to swerve designing Powerpoint presentations by doing my first one exceptionally badly! (Life hack: this same tactic also works with ironing.)

But anyway, catalogues have seemed to follow me around. The first one I had a hand in designing was the AVENT baby products catalogue, over 20 years ago. It was a small document, A5 in size, but it took the design agency where I was working months to prepare.

This was mainly because the catalogue was designed so we could cheaply produce multiple language issues just by changing the colour plate that contained all the text.

I think there were 13 language versions all told, including Hebrew and Russian. Fun fact: written German takes up 20% more space than English, which makes it tricky if you design the English version first (which, of course, we always did).

A few years later, in a new job, I ran an in-house design team producing four company catalogues (plus their language versions) each year. We were responsible for everything in them – hiring photographers and directing the photo shoots, casting models to wear our clothing, writing the words, retouching the images, creating the design and artwork – and also some of our team designed the products (mostly motorcycle clothing and accessories).

These catalogues were our brands' flagship marketing pieces, meant to showcase our whole product range for an entire year, and be distributed all over the UK, Europe and the US. So, it was important they were high quality.

After that job, I spent two years designing catalogues for Plumb Center and another kitchen and bathroom wholesaler – both as glamorous as they sound. By then, catalogue design involved linking our software to clients' sales databases to ensure accurate pricing, which seemed to make all my designer colleagues suddenly lose interest.

But I didn't mind. From showers and baby toiletries to concrete railway sleepers, electrical components and motorcycle exhausts, I have featured them all in catalogue form at some point.

Printed catalogues give your company a chance to showcase everything you do. If you do it on the cheap by designing it yourself, it shows. You don't want your business showcase to be anything less than perfect – it cheapens your brand.

If you are thinking of creating in a product catalogue, invest in the services of a designer. They can recommend a printer who prints catalogues on a regular basis, as catalogue printing is also pretty specialised. The results will be worth it.

Key Takeaways

- Catalogues are powerful marketing tools that showcase your entire product range while inspiring and persuading customers to buy.
- High-quality design, layout and photography are essential to create a professional catalogue that reflects your brand's credibility.
- Attempting a DIY approach risks producing an amateurish catalogue that can harm your brand.
- Investing in a professional designer ensures your catalogue becomes a valuable, long-lasting asset that drives sales effectively.

18

Journals

Journals are premium value-added items that can reinforce brand awareness and help differentiate your business. They also help build your reputation and serve as a tool to build loyalty and customer satisfaction.

Over the past few years, journaling has become a significant trend, capturing the attention of many who are seeking personal development and growth.

It's hard to scroll through social media or browse a self-help section without encountering someone extolling the virtues of putting pen to paper.

Regularly writing down your thoughts, as the experts suggest, can help you clarify your goals, track your progress and develop a deeper sense of self-awareness. This practice, they say, doesn't just keep you on track – it enables growth and a greater understanding of yourself and your journey.

While the concept of keeping a diary is as old as paper and handwriting itself, journaling as a modern therapeutic practice is fairly recent, taking shape in the United States during the 1960s. This period saw the rise of the self-help movement, where individuals were encouraged to take charge of their mental and emotional well-being.

Journal writing was soon recognised as a powerful tool in this process, providing a private space for reflection, problem-solving and emotional expression. The practice was no longer just about recording daily events, but a method for individuals to explore their inner worlds and cultivate personal growth.

By the 1980s, journal writing had gained such widespread popularity that it found its way into the US education system. Educators began to see the benefits of encouraging students to keep journals as part of their ongoing learning experience.

It wasn't just about improving writing skills – it was about helping young people develop critical thinking, emotional intelligence and a habit of self-reflection that could support them throughout their lives. This shift in how journals were used marked a significant moment in the practice, broadening its appeal beyond the self-help community to a much wider audience.

Fast forward to today, and the practice of journaling has expanded even further. Coaches, healers and teachers from a wide variety of disciplines now encourage the people they support to keep journals. Whether it's a weight-loss journal, a bullet journal or a gratitude journal, there seems to be a style suitable for everyone.

Each type serves a different purpose, but all share the common goal of helping individuals stay focused, motivated and engaged with their personal development journey.

With the advent of affordable digital printing and self-publishing tools, coaches can now take this practice a step further by providing their clients with original, bespoke journals tailored specifically for their programmes. These custom journals aren't just a nice thing to have – they add value to any coaching or training programme.

Coaches who offer their clients a branded, personalised journal find them a significant additional benefit to their courses, providing a tangible resource that encourages ongoing commitment and progress.

By giving clients a dedicated space to record their thoughts and reflections, coaches are offering them more than just a notebook – they're providing a powerful tool for personal growth and achievement.

The Ideal Value-Added Tool for Coaches

I've helped many coaches to publish their first journals. Some were self-designed by the coaches themselves. Another, for a fitness coach, was a 52-week fitness diary designed by me to his specifications. His journal contains space for his clients to annotate their thoughts, record their weight measurements and food intake, and it also includes motivational quotes throughout.

For another client, a management and mindset coach, I have created a series of workbooks for specific management training workshops, which are provided to all delegates of his training courses.

And I even jumped on the bandwagon to produce my own – the *Print Marketing Planning Journal* – which is a planner for small business owners which allows them to coordinate print and digital marketing planning in one place. You can purchase one from my website if you wish – *keefomatic.com/print-marketing-journal*

Journals don't cost a fortune to print and, depending on your choice of binding, order quantities start at just one copy. The journals themselves can extend to 120 pages if wire-bound, 56 pages if stitched, in sizes from A6 up to A3 on a wide range of paper stocks.

There is even an option to have the journals printed on tear-proof and wipe-clean synthetic paper – which is an ideal setup for recipe books, should you aspire to be the next Nigella.

If you are a coach, trainer or therapist, and you encourage your clients to keep a journal, why not consider creating your own and including them as a membership benefit? A well-designed journal adds a level of professionalism to your offering. It shows that you take your work seriously and that you're invested in your clients' success.

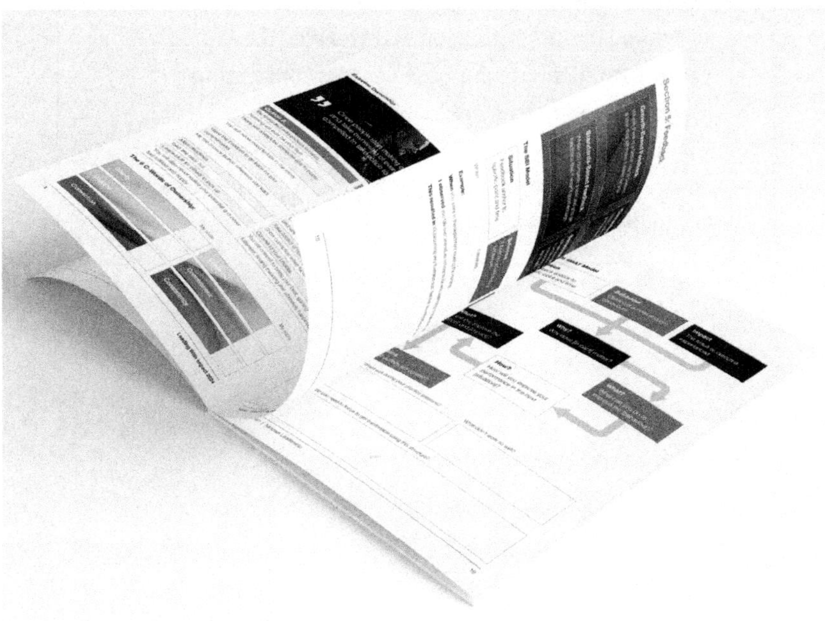

Client workbooks created for leadership development consultancy, Mindset Leadership.

For those who run training or coaching programmes, this can be particularly valuable – it's a way to differentiate yourself in a crowded market. Clients will appreciate the attention to detail, and that appreciation can translate into stronger loyalty, greater customer satisfaction and more referrals.

Key Takeaways

- Journals are a popular tool for personal development, helping individuals clarify goals, track progress and cultivate self-awareness.
- Different types of journals, such as gratitude or fitness journals, cater to specific purposes.
- Branded, bespoke journals tailored to coaching or training programmes add tangible value and reinforce client commitment.
- Affordable printing options make it easy for coaches and trainers to create custom journals, with low minimum orders and versatile formats.
- Providing clients with a journal elevates the professionalism of your services, demonstrating investment in their growth and success.
- Including a well-designed journal as part of your coaching or training package differentiates you in a competitive market.

19

Newsletters

> Newsletters keep customers engaged and informed, enhancing retention and brand awareness. They also build reputation, educate customers and can introduce new products or services.

If you talk to small business owners, as I often do, you'll hear the same objections to direct mail over and over again:

- It's too complicated.
- It doesn't work.
- It's too expensive.
- It's sleazy.

Well, here's the good news – none of that is true. In fact, if your competitors believe that, it's an even bigger opportunity for you to swoop in and grab the clients they're missing out on.

Direct mail doesn't need to be complicated. At its core, a direct mail campaign can be as simple as (1) creating an irresistible offer and (2) sending it to the right people. And one of the easiest, least "sleazy" forms of direct mail is the good old-fashioned newsletter.

You might not have ever considered writing your own newsletter, but you absolutely should. Why? Because when people are thinking about making a purchase or exploring a particular topic, they consume everything they can get their hands on – articles, podcasts, books, videos. If you can offer valuable, relevant information, they'll appreciate it, consume it and keep it for future reference. And who doesn't want to be the go-to source in their niche?

Why Newsletters Work

Regular newsletters help build strong relationships with your clients, and they sell your products or services without being pushy. It's a natural, conversational way to stay in touch and provide value, without screaming "buy from me!" Another great bonus is that the content you create for your newsletter can easily be repurposed as blog posts or social media material – a two-for-one deal!

By providing useful content regularly, you'll position yourself as the expert in your field. People will come to rely on your insights, turning to you when they need advice or solutions. Not bad for a bit of paper (or a PDF), right?

How to Get Started

OK, you get why it's a good idea – but how do you actually go about creating a newsletter? It boils down to four areas:

- Content
- Layout
- Printing
- Distribution

Content Planning

The first step is figuring out what to write. If you've ever written a blog, you might be familiar with content planning. If not, don't worry – it's easier than it sounds. Start by brainstorming all the article ideas that will interest your audience and provide them with real value.

I like to use a spreadsheet for this. In the left hand column, make a list of article types: How-Tos, Top 10 Lists, Product Reviews, News Updates, Expert Interviews, etc. Across the top row, list your key topics. If I were doing it for my business, I'd include categories like Print Design, Web Design, Marketing, Copywriting, and probably break those each into sub-categories.

Once you've got that set up, just fill in the blanks. Before you know it, you've got a matrix of potential articles like "*How to Update Your WordPress Site Without Breaking It*" or "*This Year's Top 10 Printed Marketing Must-Haves.*" From there, you can spread the articles across several months to build out a content calendar.

Then it's time to start writing! If words aren't your thing, you can get help from your team or even hire a content writer to take on the heavy lifting.

Layout

If you're confident designing it yourself, go ahead. InDesign is a great tool for laying out newsletters, but if you're a beginner, it does have a steep learning curve. Word or Canva are easier to use and come with templates to get you started. Just keep in mind, Word and Canva aren't ideal for professional printing, so if you're going for a colour newsletter with edge-to-edge images, it's worth considering professional layout software or getting help from a designer.

If you don't have the time or skills to handle the layout yourself, hiring a designer can be a worthwhile investment. They can either create a template you can use or lay out each edition for you.

Printing

The standard format for a newsletter is A3 folded to A4. Make sure you're working in multiples of four pages – one sheet of A3 paper gives you a four-page newsletter, two sheets give you eight pages, and so on. You'll supply your printer with a PDF, and they'll advise you on the best way to set up your files to avoid any printing headaches.

Distribution

Some printers offer mailing services, so they can handle everything from printing to stuffing envelopes and adding address labels. If not, you'll need to take care of envelope stuffing and postage – or get a minion to help. Before long, you'll be producing regular newsletters that stand out, build relationships and keep your customers coming back.

Newsletters as a Competitive Advantage

Newsletters are especially valuable if you run a business with a membership or subscription element. Sending a regular, well-crafted newsletter can become a part of your membership offer, adding value and even allowing you to justify a higher price. Plus, if you're smart about it, you can sell advertising space in your newsletter to cover production costs.

So, if your competitors are stuck in the "direct mail doesn't work" mindset, let them stay there. A newsletter is a simple, effective way to stand out and make sure your customers keep coming back for more.

Key Takeaways

- Newsletters build relationships and position your business as a trusted expert by keeping you in regular, non-pushy contact with clients.
- The content you create for newsletters can be repurposed for blogs or social media, doubling your marketing impact with minimal extra effort.
- They can be distributed as printed mailers or digital PDFs, offering flexibility to suit your audience and budget.
- Newsletters add value to membership or subscription services, helping you justify higher fees while keeping members engaged.
- A well-crafted newsletter helps you stand out from competitors who overlook direct mail, making it a simple way to capture attention.
- Including advertising space in your newsletters can offset production costs, making them a cost-effective marketing tool.

20

Books

Books are a strategic tool to position you as a thought leader, build awareness and educate your audience. They also help with reputation building and can support PR efforts.

Here we are, the final chapter of the book I'm writing – about print – and it's about writing your own printed book.

In other words, I'm writing about writing a book in a book that I'm writing. It's all a bit meta, don't you think? Or is it post-modern? Maybe it's something to do with the multiverse or the fourth dimension. Anyway, perhaps it's best not to dwell on it for too long, and just get on with it...

Why Write a Book?

The whole point of this book has been to help you and your business stand out by doing things other businesses don't. Most dismiss print marketing as expensive or out-of-date – and are instead lured by the bright lights and shiny promises of AI and social media. But if getting noticed is your goal, writing a book is a powerful way to do it. Many of the tactics we've covered are about boosting visibility, but books are more strategic. They're a long-term investment that can benefit your business in ways a brochure or flyer simply can't.

Here are six solid reasons why you should consider writing a book for your business:

1. A Book Establishes Your Credibility and Authority

If you want to position yourself as an expert, nothing beats having your own book. It's a giant credibility boost – a testament to your knowledge and experience. Anyone can claim to be an expert in their field, but putting your ideas into print shows you've got something worth saying. Picture your book sitting on your client's desk, silently working to keep you in their thoughts.

And it's not just for show – a well-crafted business book can open up new opportunities, like speaking engagements, consultancy gigs, podcast invitations or collaborations. It gives you a tangible edge over competitors who rely solely on the digital shout-fest of social media or do no marketing at all.

2. Books are a Long-Term Marketing Tool

Think of a book as a marketing tool with legs. Unlike a fleeting social media post or an ad that disappears as soon as the budget runs out, a book has staying power. It's a physical object that people can keep and revisit. Each chapter can spark a conversation, train new employees or serve as a giveaway that leaves a lasting impression. And if you keep it updated, you've got a timeless piece of marketing that can evolve with your business.

3. Being an Author Differentiates You from Competitors

Standing out is crucial, and a book does this better than almost anything else. It's not just about what you sell or the services you offer – it's about sharing your perspective and your approach. A book lets you dig deeper into what makes you different and why your way of doing things is special. It's like having a one-on-one conversation with your audience, giving them a better understanding of your personality, business philosophy and the unique value you bring.

4. Books Can Generate Passive Income

Now, making money might not be the main goal of your book, but it's a nice bonus. Selling your book can provide a steady income stream that adds to your primary business revenue. Plus, it can open the door to other income-generating opportunities, like workshops, seminars and paid speaking engagements that boost your bottom line.

5. Writing a Book is Good for Your Personal Development

Writing a book is no walk in the park – it takes time, discipline and plenty of reflection (trust me, I know). But the process is incredibly rewarding. It forces you to clarify your thoughts, sharpen your communication skills and become more strategic in how you present your ideas. This personal growth can translate into better business strategies, stronger leadership skills and a clearer vision for where you want to take your company.

6. A Book Leaves a Lasting Legacy
Finally, writing a book lets you leave something behind that goes beyond your business. It's a way to document your career, your lessons and your experiences for future generations. I've referenced books in this one that were written over a century ago, and their influence lives on. Your book can inspire, guide and mentor others long after you've moved on to new ventures (or to a beach somewhere). It's not just a publication – it's a record of your professional journey that can continue to make an impact.

Choosing Printed Books vs. eBooks

The hardest part of writing a book is, well, the writing. But as you get closer to finishing, you'll need to decide whether to produce a printed book, an eBook or both. This book is all about print, so you probably know where I stand! There's something powerful about a tangible book you can hold, flip through and stick on a shelf. Print has a way of creating lasting memories and emotional connections that eBooks just can't match.

I have a bookcase filled with over 250 business books. I can tell you exactly when I bought every one of them and where I was when I read them. Those books are more than just information – they're part of my professional journey. Compare that to an eBook I downloaded ages ago and now can't find or remember much about. Print books are memorable. Digital ones... not so much.

But having said that, this book is available in paperback and eBook. If your audience prefers eBooks, then by all means create one. The key is to choose the format that best suits your audience and your business goals.

The Benefits of a Hybrid Approach

While this book focuses on the power of print marketing, it's worth acknowledging that a hybrid approach – blending digital and non-digital formats – often provides the most comprehensive solution to marketing challenges. Offering both a printed book and a digital version, such as an eBook or audiobook, ensures you can meet your audience wherever they are. Some readers value the tangible, lasting impact of a printed book, while others prefer the convenience of accessing content digitally on their devices or during their commute. By catering to both preferences, you'll expand your reach and create a more inclusive offering.

The hybrid model also plays to the strengths of both formats. A printed book leaves a physical reminder of your brand, ideal for desks, bookshelves and gifts. At the same time, a digital version can provide instant accessibility, useful for customers who expect immediate downloads and convenience. Together, these formats create a marketing tool that has both staying power and adaptability, ensuring your message remains visible and accessible.

This dual approach mirrors the broader principle of integrating digital and offline marketing strategies, which I've highlighted throughout this book. Combining the emotional connection of print with the convenience and reach of digital ensures your marketing efforts are not only impactful but also versatile. In the case of your book, this means you're giving yourself the best chance to stand out - and to stick around - in an increasingly competitive environment.

Cost Considerations

For this book, I have designed, typeset and edited it myself, so my production costs are a lot lower than if you were to involve professionals. If you had to buy in professional services, the total estimated upfront costs for a book of this size range from £1,500–£4,500, including £1,000–£3,000 for editing, £300–£800 for cover design, £150–£800 for formatting and £93 for a single ISBN.

During the pre-launch phase, I was asked why there was no audiobook version available. The estimate for me to turn this into an audiobook (which I wouldn't narrate myself) was £1,000–£1,300. Assuming ambitious sales of 10 audiobooks per month (for a new author), it would take me nearly three years to recoup those production costs.

If you're considering writing a book, it's important to weigh these costs carefully before committing to the project. While the process can be rewarding, understanding the financial investment required will help you decide whether self-publishing is the right choice for your business or personal goals.

Should You Write a Book?

I have some coaches to thank for prising this book out of me. Five years ago, if you'd told me I'd be writing a book, I would have laughed. A coach of mine (hi, Vicky!) tried to talk me into it, but I wasn't having any of it. Then came the COVID lockdowns, and almost overnight, I lost most of my marketing clients. That experience made me realise that I needed to become more visible. I'd been happy working with a small group of local clients, but when that bubble popped, I realised I wasn't standing out at all.

I started by building a mailing list and sharing regular updates. I rediscovered my love of writing and, with some encouragement from another coach (thanks, Sheena!), turned those emails into a mini-series. Yet another coach (hi, Zoe!) convinced me to turn that series into something bigger, like a book or a podcast.

I didn't know much about podcasting, but I could write, so the idea of this book was born. Over 30,000 words later, here we are.

But What About You?

If you're wondering whether writing a book is right for you, it's time to ask yourself a few questions:

What unique perspective or knowledge do you have to offer?
Your book should offer something that's uniquely yours – a fresh insight, a new approach or a perspective that fills a gap in the market.

Who is your target audience?
Understanding who will read your book is crucial. Are you writing for industry peers, new entrepreneurs, potential clients or a broader audience? Knowing your audience shapes your content and tone.

How will writing a book benefit your business?
Will it enhance your credibility, attract clients or serve as a long-term marketing tool? Make sure the benefits align with your overall business strategy.

Can you commit the time and resources?
Writing a book isn't a quick project. It takes time, focus, and possibly a budget for designers, editors and marketers. Make sure you can handle it without disrupting your day-to-day operations.

How will you publish and market the book?
Are you going to self-publish, use a publisher or go digital? Each route has pros and cons, so plan ahead for distribution and promotion. You'll need a strategy for pre- to post-launch, and you'll probably need a website or a dedicated sales page.

What are your expectations from publishing?
Be clear on what success looks like. Is it all about sales, building a personal brand or attracting more business? Having realistic goals will keep you focused.

Are you prepared for feedback and criticism?
Not everyone will love your book. But if you're open to feedback, both positive and negative, it can be a valuable learning experience. After 30 years in design, I'm used to feedback – often from people who know less than I do. So I'm ready!

Ready to Take the Leap?

If you think you've got a book in you, then go for it. Whether it's to build credibility, open doors or just share your knowledge, writing a book is one of the best ways to stand up, stand out and make your mark.

Key Takeaways

- Writing a book establishes your authority and sets you apart as a credible expert.
- Books offer long-term marketing value, providing ongoing visibility and building your brand.
- They can generate passive income, create new opportunities, and deepen connections with your audience.
- The process enhances your communication skills and leaves a lasting legacy of your expertise.
- While books are powerful tools for success, it's essential to weigh the costs and effort involved before committing to the project.

Further Reading

I've mentioned a few books, authors and marketing principles throughout the book, so if you are interested in learning more, check these out for size:

How Brands Grow *by Byron Sharp*
A rather dense read, this book challenges many traditional marketing assumptions. In my introduction, I mention his argument that big brands succeed by leveraging both mental and physical availability. While these strategies are effective for large-scale brand awareness campaigns, they aren't as applicable for SMEs, who lack the budget to compete on this level. Instead, SMEs should focus on sustained marketing activity and lead generation to reach and engage their audience effectively.

The Ultimate Sales Letter *by Dan Kennedy*
Dan Kennedy's *The Ultimate Sales Letter* is a practical guide to crafting persuasive, results-driven sales letters. For SMEs, print marketing is more than just sending out flyers – it's about creating materials that convert leads into customers. Kennedy's techniques show how to structure compelling print copy that engages readers and pushes them to take immediate action, making it perfect for small business owners who want to maximise the impact of their direct mail campaigns.

The Copywriter's Handbook *by Robert W. Bly*

Robert Bly's *The Copywriter's Handbook* is a comprehensive resource for anyone looking to improve their writing skills, particularly in marketing materials. For SMEs using print marketing, this book provides valuable insights into crafting effective copy for brochures, flyers and direct mail. Bly's approach will help small business owners create clear, persuasive print content that resonates with their target audience and encourages action.

How to Write Sales Letters and Emails that Sell, and
Commonsense Direct and Digital Marketing *by Drayton Bird*

Both these books by Drayton Bird are essential reads for SMEs aiming to improve their marketing efforts across print and digital channels. With decades of experience in direct response marketing, Bird offers invaluable strategies for crafting persuasive messaging that drives sales. His practical advice focuses on understanding your audience, testing approaches and creating clear, compelling offers. Whether you're writing sales letters, designing brochures or planning email or direct mail campaigns, his techniques bridge traditional and digital marketing, helping small businesses create cohesive campaigns that deliver real results.

Scientific Advertising *by Claude Hopkins*

Claude Hopkins' *Scientific Advertising* is a timeless guide to effective advertising that's as relevant today as when it was first written over a century ago. For SMEs exploring print marketing, Hopkins' focus on testing, measuring and refining advertising efforts is crucial. His principles encourage a strategic, data-driven approach to print marketing, helping small businesses develop campaigns that are highly effective in generating leads and turning prospects into customers.

Guerilla Marketing *by Jay Conrad Levinson*

Written in 1983 and now a bit dated in places, Jay Conrad Levinson offers plenty of innovative, low-cost marketing strategies that are perfect for SMEs with limited budgets. Print marketing fits well within Levinson's framework, as it allows small businesses to reach their audience in memorable and unconventional ways. Whether it's using creative direct mail campaigns or distributing flyers in high-traffic areas, this book provides SMEs with a wealth of ideas to make their print marketing stand out without breaking the bank.

Thanks

I have the following people to thank for helping me get this book written.

Firstly, three coaches and consultants who were instrumental in encouraging/pestering me to do it: Vicky Fraser, Sheena Whyatt and Zoe Wadsworth – all of whom have pointed me in the right direction at various times, even when I had no interest in writing a book at all.

Huge thanks to my proofreaders, Jenny McIntee, Bex Elder, Sheena (again), Joanne Cooper, Rachael Chiverton, Mark Tennant, Karen Duncan and Sarah Silva – if there are any errors or typos remaining, it's all their fault!

To Anna Barker, for letting me loose marketing her garden design business for the past 17 years, which allowed me to road-test and perfect many of the tactics mentioned in the book in the real world.

I'd also like to thank all my former agency bosses, marketing managers and managing directors for believing/not believing in me *(delete as appropriate)* and for the opportunities they gave me in my early career – they set me on a path that ultimately led to this book. Those years were invaluable, teaching me the foundations of print, design and marketing, the importance of attention to detail and the value of hard-earned experience.

Thanks to all the brands whose work has been featured in the photos.

And finally, to the long-suffering subscribers of the Keefomatic mailing list, for enduring my book drivel for the last year or so.

About The Author

This is where I get to talk about myself in the third person – what fun! Here goes...

After a quarter of a century working for design agencies and in-house marketing teams – where the most exciting thing he did was direct a photoshoot on a volcano – graphic designer Keith Barker changed course in 2015 to set up his own business, *Keefomatic Marketing & Design*, a one-man agency dedicated to providing design and marketing services to small businesses.

Keith works with companies looking to grow and who understand the value that design can bring to their business.

If you'd like to know more, you can contact him directly at *keith@keefomatic.com*.

This is his first, and possibly last, book.

Printed in Great Britain
by Amazon

52635070R00076